THE CARTOON GUIDE
TO (NON) COMMUNICATION

Also by Larry Gonick

The Cartoon History of the Universe
The Cartoon History of the United States
The Cartoon Guide to the Computer
The Cartoon Guide to Genetics (with Mark Wheelis)
The Cartoon Guide to Physics (with Art Huffman)

THE CARTOON GUIDE TO (NON) COMMUNICATION

The Use and Misuse of Information in the Modern World

LARRY GONICK

HarperPerennial

A Division of HarperCollins*Publishers*

Acknowledgment

The author wishes to thank Eckart Wintzen, who orginally suggested the idea for this book and supported its development, and all the other people at BSO/Origin, for believing that a low-tech medium could help illuminate high technology.

This work was previously published in 1989 in Belgium under the title *Neo-Babelonia*.

FIRST HARPER PERENNIAL EDITION

Illustrations by Lawrence Gonick

Trademark symbols shown on page 131 are the property of AT&T, the Hearst Corporation and Merrill Lynch & Co., Inc.

Library of Congress Cataloging-in-Publication Data

Gonick, Larry.
  [Neo-Babelonia]
  The cartoon guide to (non) communication : the use and misuse of information in the modern world / Larry Gonick.
      p.   cm.
  Originally published: Neo-Babelonia. Belgium, 1989.
  Includes index.
  ISBN 0-06-273217-X
  1. Communication—Caricatures and cartoons.   I. Title
P91.G626   1993
741.5′973—dc20   92-54433

93 94 95 96 97 LG/RRD 10 9 8 7 6 5 4 3 2

CONTENTS

⟨ INTRODUCTION ⟩

YOU ALL KNOW THE STORY OF THE *TOWER OF BABEL* (DON'T YOU?): SOME OVER-AMBITIOUS IRAQI ARCHITECTS DESIGN A TEMPLE SO TALL, A CONVERSATION WITH HEAVEN WOULD BE A LOCAL CALL...

GOD, IN HIS PIQUE, SMITES THE WORKERS WITH A PLAGUE OF FOREIGN LANGUAGES, AND THE PROJECT PETERS OUT.

DESPITE THE CONFUSION, TECHNOLOGY MARCHED ON... AND SO WE'VE BEEN BLESSED WITH A COMMUNICATION PROBLEM THAT MAKES THE BIBLICAL BABEL SOUND LIKE THE ESPERANTO SOCIETY!!

NOW, IN ADDITION TO SO-CALLED "NATURAL" LANGUAGES SUCH AS FRENCH, ENGLISH, CHINESE, TURKISH, SUMERIAN AND UGARITIC, WE ALSO HAVE:

WELL, IT'S OBVIOUS, THE BIBLE WAS RIGHT...

TODAY WE'RE SURROUNDED BY "COMMUNICATIONS TECHNOLOGY"— COPIERS, FAXES, LASER PRINTERS, CAR PHONES, AUTODIALERS, E-MAIL... YES, SURROUNDED IT IS !!

DON'T GET ME WRONG...I LOVE THIS STUFF! I CAN FAX BELGIUM IN A MINUTE... E-MAIL ANYPLACE WITH A LOCAL CALL...GET ACCESS TO INFORMATION 1 NEVER DREAMED OF... WASTE HOURS AND HOURS "COMMUNICATING !!"

BUT SOMETIMES YOU HAVE TO WONDER: IS ALL THIS MANIPULATION
AND TRANSMISSION OF INFORMATION REALLY COMMUNICATION?
OR ITS OPPOSITE? INFORMATION WE DON'T NEED, PEOPLE WE CAN'T
SEE, JARGON WE CAN'T UNDERSTAND, MOTIVES WE CAN'T ASSESS,
FEELINGS WE CAN'T FATHOM...

IN THIS BOOK, WE'RE GOING TO EXPLORE SOME OF THE WAYS
TECHNOLOGY INTERFERES WITH COMMUNICATION.
OUR GUIDE
WILL BE THE
INCOMPARABLE

C. ARTHUR TOON.

WE'LL START WITH THE INVENTION OF THE SPOKEN WORD ITSELF, SO OFTEN USED TO DECEIVE, DISGUISE, AND DISTORT.

WE'LL CONSIDER THE ART OF WRITING... THE ROLE OF LOGIC... THE IMAGING TECHNOLOGIES OF PAINTING, PHOTOGRAPHY, VIDEO, AND VIRTUAL REALITY... AND OF COURSE, THE SEDUCTIVE COMPUTER!

AND ALL ALONG, WE ASK: HOW DOES COMMUNICATION SATISFY OUR **EMOTIONAL** NEEDS? WHAT ARE ITS BIOLOGICAL AND CULTURAL ROOTS? WHAT IS HUMANLY APPROPRIATE? HOW CAN WE USE TECHNOLOGY TO SHARE KNOWLEDGE AND MEANING, RATHER THAN SPREAD MANIPULATION, ANXIETY, AND CONFUSION??

PART ONE
◇ LANGUAGE ◇

"HOW CAN YOU TALK WITH
A PERSON IF THEY ALWAYS
SAY THE SAME THING?"

—ALICE THROUGH
THE LOOKING GLASS

· CHAPTER 1 ·
REPTILE ROOTS

IN THE BEGINNING WAS
THE WORD...

AND THE WORD WAS —

EVER SINCE THE DAWN OF TIME,
THERE HAS BEEN COMMUNICATION,
AND COMMUNICATION HAS
EXPRESSED ORGANIC NEEDS.

CHEMICAL
SIGNALS

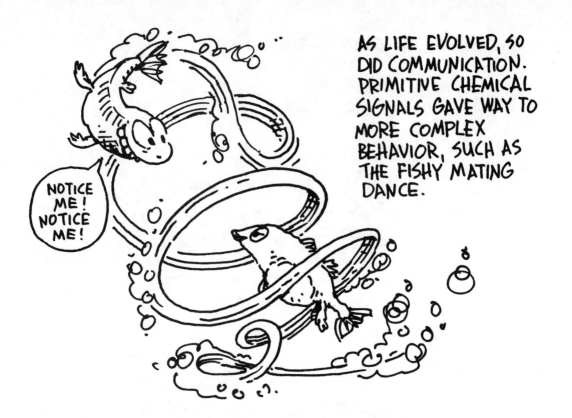

AS LIFE EVOLVED, SO DID COMMUNICATION. PRIMITIVE CHEMICAL SIGNALS GAVE WAY TO MORE COMPLEX BEHAVIOR, SUCH AS THE FISHY MATING DANCE.

NOTICE ME! NOTICE ME!

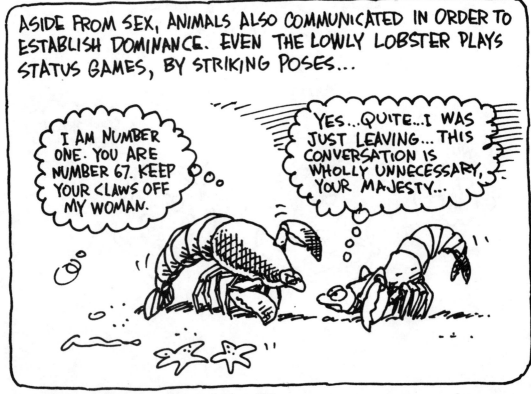

ASIDE FROM SEX, ANIMALS ALSO COMMUNICATED IN ORDER TO ESTABLISH DOMINANCE. EVEN THE LOWLY LOBSTER PLAYS STATUS GAMES, BY STRIKING POSES...

I AM NUMBER ONE. YOU ARE NUMBER 67. KEEP YOUR CLAWS OFF MY WOMAN.

YES...QUITE...I WAS JUST LEAVING...THIS CONVERSATION IS WHOLLY UNNECESSARY, YOUR MAJESTY...

HOW OFTEN IS HUMAN SPEECH
A MERE EMBELLISHMENT OF BASIC,
PRIMITIVE, LOBSTER "BODY LANGUAGE?"

ANYWAY... THE LUNGFISH WRIGGLED ONTO THE BEACH, AND COMMUNICATION BECAME AIRBORNE.

WE'RE FAMILIAR WITH BIRDS CALLING, FROGS CROAKING, AND OTHER EXAMPLES OF ANIMAL COMMUNICATION — ALL EXPRESSING PHYSICAL NEEDS.

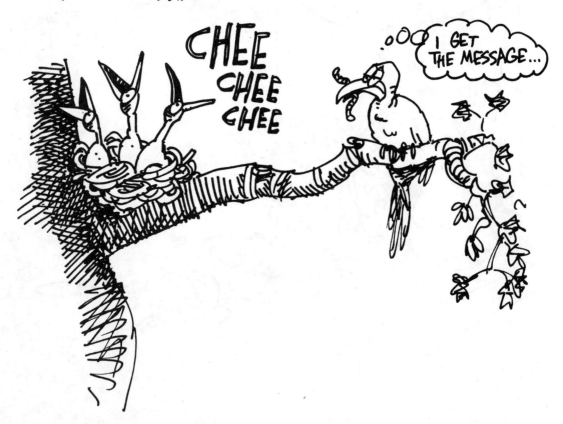

GRADUALLY, THE RANGE OF SUBJECTS TO BE COMMUNICATED EXPANDED... THE BRAIN DEVELOPED... AND AROUND 250 MILLION YEARS AGO CAME AN ESSENTIAL STEP IN OUR EVOLUTION: THE "REPTILE BRAIN," A BRAIN THAT RESPONDED TO THE OUTSIDE WORLD BY TRIGGERING THE PHYSIOLOGICAL RESPONSES WE KNOW AS THE **EMOTIONS.**

APPARENTLY, THOSE DINOSAURS WERE EMOTIONAL CREATURES — AT LEAST, I'D LIKE TO THINK SO...

NOW WE MAMMALS BEGAN AS A KIND OF HAIRY REPTILE.

BUT DID OUR BRILLIANT, EVOLVED BRAINS EVER ESCAPE FROM THEIR OLD-FASHIONED, OBSOLETE REPTILIAN ROOTS ??

SAY "AH..."

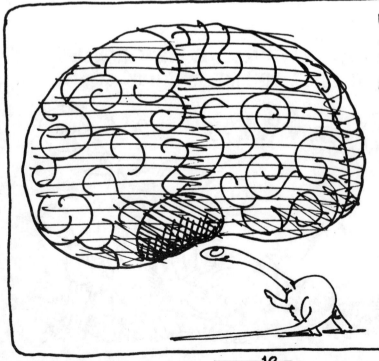

NOT A BIT! WE JUST COVERED IT UP WITH A MOUNTAIN OF "HIGHER" BRAIN CELLS... BUT THE OLD REPTILE BRAIN IS STILL DOWN THERE, CHURNING OUT EMOTIONS! (ITS PROPER SCIENTIFIC NAME IS "LIMBIC SYSTEM," BY THE WAY.)

THE LIMBIC SYSTEM IS RESPONSIBLE FOR OUR BASIC EMOTIONAL RESPONSES.

IT CAN BE TRIGGERED BY A SIGHT, A SOUND, A SMELL, OR A WORD OR A MEMORY.

THE REPTILE BRAIN SIGNALS YOUR BODY TO GO INTO A HEIGHTENED STATE...

PANT PANT!!

POUND POUND

YOU CAN'T STOP THE RESPONSE! IT'S AUTOMATIC!! AT BEST, YOU CAN DEAL WITH IT ONLY AFTER IT'S ALREADY HAPPENING!!

BE COOL. SHOW NOTHING...

YES, WE ALL HAVE A DINOSAUR INSIDE, TRYING TO GET OUT!

BUT EXPRESSING YOUR REPTILE IS BAD MANNERS! AFTER ALL, IT'S THAT HIGHER BRAIN THAT MAKES US HUMAN... SO WE HAVE DEVELOPED AN AMAZING HABIT: WE IGNORE OUR EMOTIONS...

MY POINT IS THIS: THE LANGUAGE THAT COMES OUT OF OUR MOUTHS CAN BE INCIDENTAL TO THE CONTENT OF OUR COMMUNICATION.

REJECT ME, WILL YOU? DRAGON!

HA HA

POLITICS

GOSSIP

RECIPES

REAL ESTATE

WHY DO I FEEL WEIRD NOW?

IF YOU DIDN'T TALK SO MUCH, YOU WOULD KNOW!

BUT WE'RE SO FOCUSED ON VERBIAGE, WE IMAGINE SPEECH EXPRESSES MEANING— EVEN WHEN IT REALLY IS USED TO DISGUISE MEANING.

THIS IS A (LARGELY UNACKNOWLEDGED) PROBLEM WITH COMPUTER UNDERSTANDING OF NATURAL LANGUAGE. EVEN IF THE COMPUTER "GOT IT," IT WOULDN'T GET IT!! COMPUTERS HAVE NO DINOSAUR INSIDE!!!*

SPEAK TO ME!!

*YET!

21

A GOOD EXAMPLE IS THIS CONVERSATION I OVERHEARD IN THE SUPERMARKET THE OTHER DAY. IT WAS SPOKEN IN A COMPLETELY FLAT, UNEMOTIONAL VOICE.

WHAT WAS THIS CONVERSATION ABOUT? THE INFORMATION EXCHANGED WAS SEEMINGLY USELESS... NOTHING PRACTICAL WAS COMMUNICATED, AT LEAST OVERTLY... YET NEITHER PARTY SEEMED TO THINK IT WAS STRANGE OR CONFUSING.

NO QUESTION ABOUT IT, THE **REAL** CONVERSATION TOOK PLACE AT THE REPTILE LEVEL. TRANSLATION:

THE EMOTIONAL ROOTS OF LANGUAGE GO VERY DEEP. OF COURSE, IT IS IMPOSSIBLE TO GO BACK IN TIME TO THE ORIGIN OF HUMAN SPEECH, BUT THIS HASN'T STOPPED ANYONE FROM SPECULATING ON THE NATURE OF EARLY SPEECH.

THE STANDARD THEORY IS THAT HUMAN LANGUAGE IS ELABORATED ANIMAL COMMUNICATION, GROWN COMPLEX ENOUGH TO EXPRESS OUR INTELLIGENCE AND DESCRIBE OUR LIVES.

ANOTHER IDEA, ADVANCED BY S. LANGER,* IS THAT LANGUAGE BEGAN AS AN EMOTIONAL ACT— AN EXPRESSION OF EXCESS FEELING, WHICH RESONATED IN THE HEARTS OF THE LISTENERS.

*IN MIND: AN ESSAY ON HUMAN FEELING, BALTIMORE, MD., JOHNS HOPKINS PRESS, 1973.

MY FAVORITE HISTORICAL EXAMPLE IS A RITUAL PERFORMED ANNUALLY BY THE SPARTANS, BACK IN ANCIENT GREECE.

THE SPARTANS LIVED A LIFE OF STRICT SELF-DENIAL... THEY TOLERATED NO DISSENT... SO IT WAS ESSENTIAL THAT EVERY SPARTAN KNOW THE LAW.

READY?

SO EVERY YEAR, THE SPARTANS HELD A FESTIVAL, AT WHICH THE ENTIRE POPULACE CHANTED THE LAW CODE !!

"CRIMINAL CODE, SECTION ONE, PARAGRAPH 8"...

THIS IS CALLED "GETTING IT RIGHT."

A MODERN EXAMPLE WOULD BE THE **WEDDING** CEREMONY.
THE RITUAL OF THE WEDDING SERVES SEVERAL PURPOSES
(TO MAKE A PRIVATE ACT PUBLIC, TO UNITE TWO FAMILIES, TO
BEGGAR THE BRIDE'S PARENTS), ONE OF WHICH IS SURELY TO
ACT ON THE COUPLE'S **INNER REPTILES.**

THE SIMPLE WORDS, "I DO," HAVE A POWERFUL
HARMONIZING EFFECT!!

THERE IS PROBABLY SOME TRUTH IN BOTH IDEAS. IT IS IMPOSSIBLE TO SEPARATE PRACTICAL NEEDS FROM EMOTIONAL STATES. ALL THE CONCERNS OF PRIMITIVE PEOPLE HAVE THIS DUAL NATURE: OBJECTIVE PROBLEMS WITH A SUBJECTIVE CHARGE:

HUNTING/FISHING
GATHERING
DEATH
BIRTH
KINSHIP
TECHNOLOGY
HOUSE-BUILDING
EATING
THE WEATHER
SEX
STATUS
THE UNKNOWN

TAKE HUNTING, FOR EXAMPLE. IT INVOLVES SOME OBVIOUS PRACTICAL PROBLEMS, TO WHICH LANGUAGE MAY REFER.

WHAT WE HUNT?

SABER-TOOTH TIGER!

WHO'S GOING?

NOT ME!

...BUT THE UNIQUELY HUMAN ASPECT OF THE HUNT IS THE EMOTIONAL SENSE OF
PRIDE IN TEAMWORK,
AWE AT THE POWER OF NATURE,
KINSHIP WITH THE HUNTED ANIMAL, AND THE MYSTERY OF LIFE AND DEATH —
THAT SORT OF THING!

GET OUT THE DRUMS AND WHISTLES!

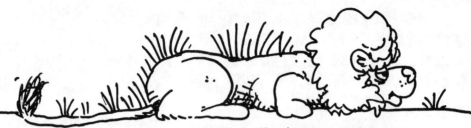

AFTER ALL, THE LION, A GREAT HUNTER, DOES ITS JOB WITHOUT BENEFIT OF LANGUAGE (OR AT LEAST A LANGUAGE ANYTHING LIKE OURS). NO, WHAT SEPARATES HUMAN HUNTERS FROM THE LION IS PRECISELY THE HUMAN'S COMPLEX EXPRESSION OF EMOTION — IN THE FORM OF **RITUAL.**

WHEREVER YOU FIND PEOPLE, YOU FIND RITUAL... YOU FIND HUNTERS DOING A DANCE WEARING A LION MASK.

WHEN WAS THE LAST TIME YOU SAW A LION WEARING A HUMAN MASK?

SIGH WE HAVE NOTHING TO TALK ABOUT.

OUR EMOTIONAL NEEDS HAVE LED PEOPLE IN EVERY CULTURE TO INVENT RITUALS FOR HUNTING, PLANTING, HARVESTING, BIRTH, DEATH, MARRIAGE, HOUSE·BUILDING, TOOL-MAKING, ETC ETC ETC...

IN THE SPEECH AND ACTIONS OF RITUAL, WE UNIFY OUR EMOTIONAL RESPONSES WITH OUR FELLOW HUMANS... WE AGREE ON THE MEANING OF OUR COMMON EXPERIENCE... AND WE CONCLUDE THAT THE MOST EFFECTIVE COMMUNICATION COMBINES **LANGUAGE AND ACTION.**

·CHAPTER 2·
UNDERSTANDING
UNDERSTANDING

THIS IS A BOOK ABOUT LANGUAGE, SO I WOULD BE REMISS IF I DIDN'T USE A FEW REALLY **BIG WORDS**... WITHOUT FURTHER ADO, THEN, HERE ARE THREE WHOPPERS:

KINESTHETIC
ICONIC
SYMBOLIC

(AND, THIS BEING ALSO A BOOK ABOUT IMAGES, I CAN MAKE THE WORDS **VISUALLY** LARGE, AS WELL AS CONCEPTUALLY HEAVY.)

WORDS OF HEIGHT **AND** WEIGHT!

AS USED BY THE CHILD PSYCHOLOGIST **JEROME BRUNER,** THE TERMS KINESTHETIC, ICONIC, AND SYMBOLIC REFERRED TO STAGES IN CHILDREN'S MENTAL DEVELOPMENT, FROM THE CONCRETE TO THE ABSTRACT... BUT WE CAN ALSO DESCRIBE ADULT THINKING IN EXACTLY THE SAME WORDS.

KINESTHETIC KNOWLEDGE IS WHAT WE LEARN BY DOING. THE OTHER TWO ARE ULTIMATELY BASED ON KINESTHETIC KNOWLEDGE —

 FOR EXAMPLE, THE HUMAN MIND CAN MENTALLY ROTATE IMAGES. THIS IS A SKILL WE LEARN IN CHILDHOOD FROM THE EXPERIENCE OF TURNING OBJECTS AROUND WITH OUR HANDS.

AS ADULTS, WE HAVE RISEN ABOVE THE PURELY KINESTHETIC LEVEL...

YES, WE ARE UNIQUELY BRILLIANT, CLEVER, AND MODEST.

BUT OUR LANGUAGE CONTINUES TO REVEAL ITS IMPORTANCE:

WHEN WE UNDERSTAND A CONCEPT, WE SAY WE "GRASP IT... WE "GET A HANDLE" ON AN IDEA... AS FOR INFORMATION, WE "HANDLE" OR "MANIPULATE" IT — ALL WORDS DERIVED FROM HAND, OUR MOST IMPORTANT INFORMATION PROCESSOR!

CAREFUL!

CONSEQUENTLY, WHAT WE **DO** VERY MUCH AFFECTS THE WAY WE **THINK**... AS ILLUSTRATED BY THE FOLLOWING FABLE, WHICH I CALL "TWO GUYS, ONE STICK."

TWO GUYS, ONE STICK

THE MORAL OF THIS STORY IS THAT WHAT WE MEAN BY A WORD DEPENDS ON WHAT OUR EXPERIENCE OF IT HAS BEEN... OUR UNDERSTANDING DEPENDS ON OUR BACKGROUND... EXPERIENCE IS A GREAT TEACHER... "HANDS-ON" INSTRUCTION IS INDISPENSIBLE... A MEETING OF THE MINDS DEPENDS ON SHARED EXPERIENCE.

ET CETERA.

IN OTHER WORDS, THINGS LOOK DIFFERENT AT OPPOSITE ENDS OF THE STICK.

STICK? AN EXCELLENT MANAGEMENT TOOL, ESPECIALLY WHEN COUPLED WITH A CARROT!!

STICK? STICK OW!

ICONIC

UNDERSTANDING IS THE LEVEL WE
REACH WHEN EXPERIENCE BEGINS
TO REVEAL SIMILARITIES, GENERALIZATIONS,
ANALOGIES ...

THE WORD "ICONIC" REFERS
TO THE FACT THAT WE
OFTEN REALIZE THESE
RELATIONSHIPS IN VISUAL
TERMS, AS ICONS.

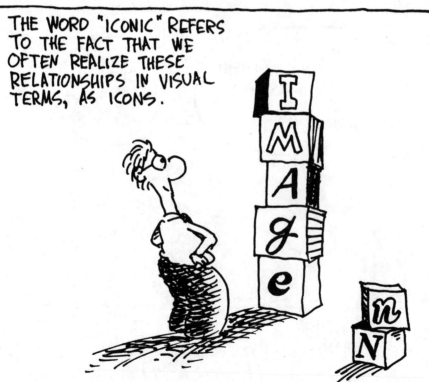

FOR A SIMPLE EXAMPLE, LOOK AT HOUSES. HOUSES CAN BE TALL OR SHORT, BIG OR SMALL, BUILT OF BRICK OR STONE OR THATCH OR MAMMOTH IVORY OR WOOD... BUT WE CHOOSE (SOMETIMES) TO IGNORE THEIR DIFFERENCES, AND GROUP THEM ALL TOGETHER UNDER THE HEADING "HOUSE..." WHICH, IF YOU THINK ABOUT IT, YOU PROBABLY ASSOCIATE WITH AN ICON THAT LOOKS LIKE THIS:

ICON OF A HOUSE

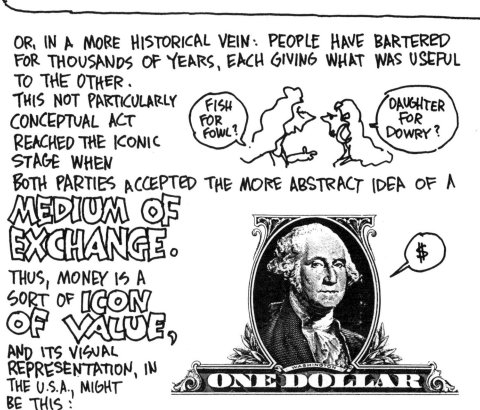

OR, IN A MORE HISTORICAL VEIN: PEOPLE HAVE BARTERED FOR THOUSANDS OF YEARS, EACH GIVING WHAT WAS USEFUL TO THE OTHER.

THIS NOT PARTICULARLY CONCEPTUAL ACT REACHED THE ICONIC STAGE WHEN

FISH FOR FOWL?

DAUGHTER FOR DOWRY?

BOTH PARTIES ACCEPTED THE MORE ABSTRACT IDEA OF A

MEDIUM OF EXCHANGE.

THUS, MONEY IS A SORT OF **ICON OF VALUE**, AND ITS VISUAL REPRESENTATION, IN THE U.S.A., MIGHT BE THIS:

$

ONE DOLLAR

OR, GOING EVEN FARTHER BACK,
TO THE STONE AGE... TOOL-MAKING
WAS PROBABLY KINESTHETIC AT
FIRST... A SERIES OF INSTRUCTIONS:

FIND A GOOD ROCK...

WHACK IT WITH ANOTHER ROCK...

CHOP

SHAPE THE FLAKES... SHARPEN THE EDGES...

CHIP CHIP CHIP

BANDAGE FINGER.

ETC...

BUT! AT SOME POINT, WITHIN THE PAST 40,000 YEARS, TOOL-MAKING BECAME ICONIC. OUR ANCESTORS BEGAN CRAFTING "IDEAL" SPEARPOINTS, PERFECT FORMS, WHOSE ONLY "POINT" WAS TO SOLIDIFY THE CONCEPT TOWARD WHICH ALL GOOD SPEARPOINT MAKERS WERE STRIVING: AN ICON OF A SPEARPOINT!!

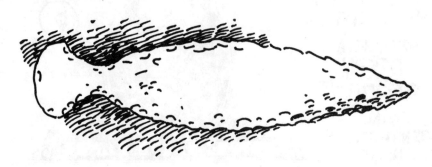

THE PREHISTORIC PLATO WHO MADE IDEAL SPEAR POINTS WAS NOT ALONE. AROUND 35,000 YEARS AGO, WE ALSO FIND THE EARLIEST EXAMPLES OF **ART**: ANIMAL AND HUMAN (USUALLY FEMALE) FIGURINES.

(DRAWING DID NOT BEGIN UNTIL MUCH LATER...)

THE EXPERTS, WHO ARE NOT BASHFUL ABOUT SPECULATING ABOUT THESE THINGS, SEE THIS EARLY ART AS REPRESENTING A NEW STAGE OF HUMAN UNDERSTANDING.

IT'S ICONIC!

THE EARLY ARTISTS ABSTRACTED THE QUALITIES OF ONE THING AND REPRODUCED THEM IN ANOTHER MEDIUM — AN ESSENTIAL STEP IN THE EVOLUTION OF LANGUAGE, THE INVENTION OF POETRY, AND THE USE OF **METAPHOR**.

YOU'RE A BEAR, DARLING!

YOU EAT GRUBS AND SLEEP ALL WINTER.

AWWW, SHUCKS!

THE IDEA OF ICONS BURST INTO PUBLIC AWARENESS WITH THE *MACINTOSH COMPUTER* AND ITS WIDELY IMITATED *GRAPHIC USER INTERFACE*, OR *GUI*. THE GUI DISPLAYS AN ASSORTMENT OF ICONS, WHICH THE USER SELECTS BY MEANS OF A MOBILE POINTING DEVICE, OR MOUSE. SUDDENLY, THE COMPUTER IS CONNECTED TO THE USER'S BASIC LEVELS OF UNDERSTANDING: SEE, POINT, CLICK.

SOME OF MY FAVORITE ICONS:

 COFFEE CUP (I STILL DON'T KNOW WHAT IT MEANS!)

 TRASH CAN FOR DELETING FILES

 BURIED CADILLAC FOR SYSTEM CRASHES (ON SILICON GRAPHICS IRIS COMPUTERS)

 AND HOW DO YOU MAKE AN ICON OF AN ICON?

AND NOW AT LAST WE COME TO

SYMBOLIC

THINKING.

WHAT'S THE DIFFERENCE BETWEEN A SYMBOL AND AN ICON?

A SYMBOL IS AN ICON WITH AN ATTITUDE.

IN EVERYDAY SPEECH, THERE IS LITTLE DIFFERENCE BETWEEN A SYMBOL AND AN ICON. IS THE DOLLAR AN ICON OF VALUE OR A SYMBOL OF VALUE?

BUT THERE ARE DIFFERENCES! THE FIRST ONE IS THAT A SYMBOL IS A HIGHER-LEVEL ABSTRACTION THAN AN ICON. AN ICON VISIBLY EXPRESSES SOME "GROUND-LEVEL" RELATIONSHIP. A SYMBOL CAN STAND FOR A RELATIONSHIP BETWEEN ICONS, A RELATIONSHIP BETWEEN RELATIONSHIPS... ETC. AD INFINITUM AND AD NAUSEAM!

BEGINNING WITH MONEY, FOR EXAMPLE, WE GENERALIZE TO CONCEPTS SYMBOLIZED BY SUCH WORDS AS CAPITAL, PRICE, WAGE, SAVINGS, GROSS NATIONAL PRODUCT, TAXATION, TARIFF BARRIERS, NATIONAL ECONOMY, ECONOMICS, ECONOMIC THEORY, MACROECONOMICS, MICROECONOMICS, ECONOMETRICS, INPUT-OUTPUT MODELING...

YES... WE'VE LEFT EARTH...

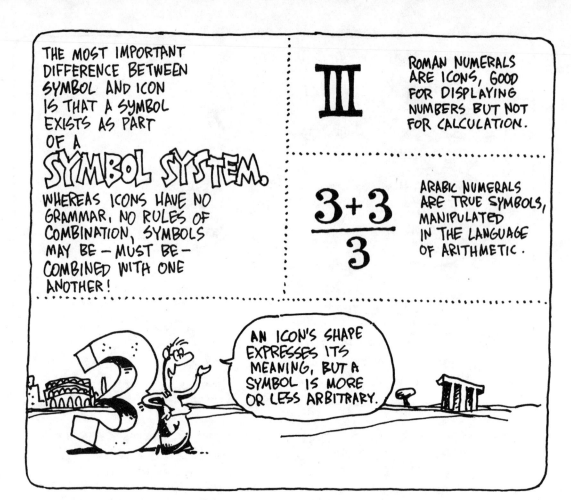

THE MOST IMPORTANT DIFFERENCE BETWEEN SYMBOL AND ICON IS THAT A SYMBOL EXISTS AS PART OF A **SYMBOL SYSTEM.** WHEREAS ICONS HAVE NO GRAMMAR, NO RULES OF COMBINATION, SYMBOLS MAY BE — MUST BE — COMBINED WITH ONE ANOTHER!

ROMAN NUMERALS ARE ICONS, GOOD FOR DISPLAYING NUMBERS BUT NOT FOR CALCULATION.

$$\frac{3+3}{3}$$

ARABIC NUMERALS ARE TRUE SYMBOLS, MANIPULATED IN THE LANGUAGE OF ARITHMETIC.

AN ICON'S SHAPE EXPRESSES ITS MEANING, BUT A SYMBOL IS MORE OR LESS ARBITRARY.

COMPLICATED COMBINATIONS OF RARIFIED RELATIONS — GREAT!!

ERGONOMIC ECONOMETRIC HYPER-GEOMETRIC MODELING, NECESSITATING INTENSIVE RETROADJUSTMENT OF HYPERBOLIC HOMEO-STATIC DISEQUILI-BRIATION. YOU AGREE OF COURSE?

VERB?

SO HOW COME WE'RE SO GOOD AT IT??

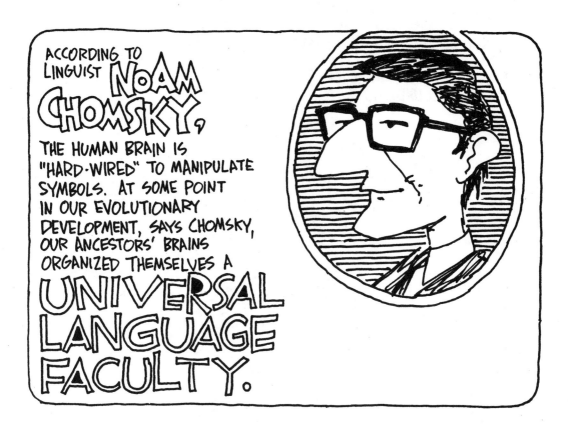

ACCORDING TO LINGUIST **NOAM CHOMSKY**, THE HUMAN BRAIN IS "HARD-WIRED" TO MANIPULATE SYMBOLS. AT SOME POINT IN OUR EVOLUTIONARY DEVELOPMENT, SAYS CHOMSKY, OUR ANCESTORS' BRAINS ORGANIZED THEMSELVES A **UNIVERSAL LANGUAGE FACULTY.**

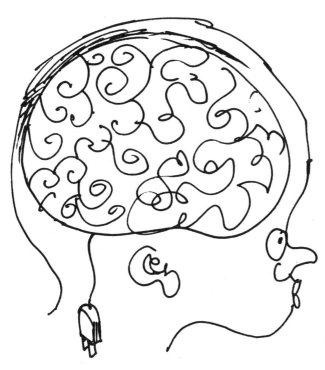

CHOMSKY SEES IN ALL LANGUAGES THE SAME "DEEP GRAMMAR," DESPITE SUPERFICIAL DIFFERENCES. WE ARE ALL WIRED THE SAME!

IN ANCIENT TIMES, PEOPLE USED THEIR NEW-FOUND SYMBOLIC PROWESS TO WEAVE MYTHS THAT EXPLAINED THEIR ICONIC WORLD.

... AND TODAY, WORDS ARE INDISPENSIBLE FOR CONVEYING HEAPS OF ESSENTIAL INFORMATION.

WE ARE SUCH EXPERTS AT UNDERSTANDING LANGUAGE THAT WE TAKE OUR OWN SKILL FOR GRANTED. YET ISN'T IT AMAZING THAT WE IMMEDIATELY UNDERSTAND TWO SENTENCES LIKE THESE (THE LINGUISTS' FAVORITE EXAMPLE):

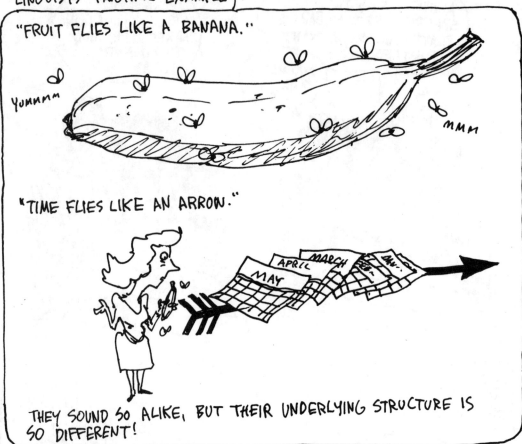

"FRUIT FLIES LIKE A BANANA."

YUMMMM

MMM

"TIME FLIES LIKE AN ARROW."

APRIL MARCH MAY

MAY

THEY SOUND SO ALIKE, BUT THEIR UNDERLYING STRUCTURE IS SO DIFFERENT!

(ACTUALLY, THE FIRST SENTENCE IS DELIGHTFULLY AMBIGUOUS. IT COULD REFER TO THE CULINARY PREFERENCES OF THE FRUIT FLY — DROSOPHILA MELANOGASTER — OR IT MIGHT DESCRIBE THE AFTERMATH OF A BAD CONCERT...)

I DIDN'T KNOW BANANAS COULD FLY, UNTIL NOW...

IN EITHER CASE, WE "GET IT.

48

NOUNS INTO VERBS? VERBS INTO NOUNS? NO PROBLEM!!

"FLIES LIKE A COOL BREEZE."

REFRESHING!

"TIME FLIES LIKE A COOL BREEZE."

I'M LATE!

"THEY TIME FLIES LIKE A COOL BREEZE."

ANNUAL FLY RACE

ZUM

(ADMITTEDLY, THAT LAST ONE MAKES HARDLY ANY SENSE — BUT IT IS GRAMMATICAL!)

YOU CAN VERB ANY WORD IN THE LANGUAGE!

EACH OF THESE SENTENCES SITS INSIDE THE NEXT ONE... BUT WE CAN SHIFT FROM ONE TO ANOTHER WITHOUT GETTING LOST. PRETTY CLEVER, AREN'T WE ??

TO APPRECIATE FULLY HOW AMAZING WE ARE, YOU HAVE ONLY TO LOOK AT HOW SUCCESSFUL THE COMPUTER IS AT UNDERSTANDING "NATURAL" LANGUAGE. HOW WELL DOES OUR MOST INTELLIGENT MACHINE DO, WHEN IT COMES TO MANIPULATING ENGLISH, DUTCH, FRENCH, JAPANESE, OR RUSSIAN IN ANY INTELLIGENT WAY? IN TWO WORDS:

IT'S NOT A HARDWARE PROBLEM, BUT A SOFTWARE PROBLEM.

(IN THEORY, A COMPUTER CAN SIMULATE ANYTHING, GIVEN THE RIGHT SOFTWARE!)

BUT LANGUAGE IS MYSTERIOUS AND COMPLICATED! SOFTWARE DESIGNERS ARE STILL GROPING FOR WAYS TO REPRESENT THE FUZZY, SQUISHY, METAPHORICAL, IMPRECISE, YET IMMENSELY USEFUL PHENOMENON OF "NATURAL" LANGUAGE IN THE FORMAL LANGUAGE OF A COMPUTER PROGRAM— IN SHORT, TO BRIDGE THE GULF BETWEEN LOGIC AND MEANING.

50

·CHAPTER 3·
IS LANGUAGE LOGICAL ?

IS LANGUAGE LOGICAL?
THE LOGICAL ANSWER
WOULD HAVE TO BE
YES OR NO.

YES OR NO...
I LIKE THE
SOUND OF
THAT...

(A LOGICIAN)

BUT THE ILLOGICAL — AND TRUE — ANSWER IS
"YES **AND** NO." LANGUAGE CAN BE LOGICAL, BUT
LANGUAGE CAN ALSO BE MESSY, AMBIGUOUS, VAGUE,
APPROXIMATE, PROBABILISTIC, EMOTIONAL, BEAUTIFUL,
POETIC, AND SEVERAL OTHER THINGS YOU CAN PROBABLY
THINK OF...

THERE, THERE..
IT'S O.K...
IT'S REALLY
MORE USEFUL
THIS WAY...

THINK ABOUT LOGIC FOR A MINUTE... THE FIRST THING YOU NOTICE ABOUT LOGIC IS—

THAT IT MAKES ME EXTREMELY UNCOMFORTABLE?

O.K... THE *SECOND* THING ABOUT LOGIC IS THAT EVERY STATEMENT IN LOGIC IS EITHER

TRUE OR FALSE.

FOR EXAMPLE, THE STATEMENT, "ALL CROWS ARE BLACK."

AT WHAT TEMPERATURE?

ALREADY LOGIC IS UNREAL! CAN WE REALLY DIVIDE THE WORLD CLEANLY INTO THE BLACK AND THE *NON·BLACK*? WHAT ABOUT THE GRAYS? WHAT ABOUT "METAPHORICAL" BLACK? IS A "BLACK" MOOD BLACK? WHAT ABOUT THE PANTS I AM WEARING TODAY? I SAY THEY'RE BLACK, BUT MY WIFE INSISTS THEY'RE DARK BLUE! WHAT DOES A LOGICIAN SAY?

TAKE THEM OFF.

IF YOU'RE SURE IT WILL HELP...

AND, EVEN IF ALL CROWS ARE BLACK, HOW CAN WE KNOW IT? SUDDENLY WE'RE IN DEEP PHILOSOPHICAL WATER!

WHAT IS PHILOSOPHY?

YOU'RE STANDING IN IT!

CONSIDER FOR A MOMENT HOW WE KNOW THE TRUTH OF A STATEMENT LIKE "ALL CROWS ARE BLACK." WE DO IT BY ACCUMULATING EVIDENCE — BY CROW-WATCHING, FOR EXAMPLE. EVERY BLACK CROW WE SEE IS FURTHER EVIDENCE OF THE TRUTH.

BUT

A) "ALL CROWS ARE BLACK" IS EQUIVALENT TO

B) "ALL NON-BLACK THINGS ARE NOT CROWS."

THE TRUTH OF ONE IS THE SAME AS THE TRUTH OF THE OTHER. SO LET'S LOOK FOR EVIDENCE TO SUPPORT STATEMENT B).

EVERY TIME WE SEE A RED APPLE, BLUEBERRY, BROWN DOG,

OR ANY OTHER NON-BLACK NON-CROW...

IT IS ALSO EVIDENCE THAT— ALL CROWS ARE BLACK!!?!

HOW DID WE TALK OURSELVES INTO **THIS** ONE?

WITH PURE LOGIC.

NOTHING ILLUSTRATES THE
DIFFERENCE BETWEEN LANGUAGE
AND LOGIC BETTER THAN THE
LITTLE, THREE-LETTER
WORD **not.**

IN LOGIC, "NOT" EFFECTS A COMPLETE REVERSAL. TRUE
BECOMES FALSE — VERY NOT-COMPLEX!

BUT IN LIFE — OH, LA! WHAT HAPPENS WHEN I WRITE: "DO **NOT**
IMAGINE A HIPPOPOTAMUS WITH A SCOOP OF ICE CREAM
IN EACH EAR"? OOPS!

DESPITE ITS SUPPOSED MEANING, "NOT" CAN BE A SMALL WORD
ATTACHED TO A BIG IDEA. IT'S
ESPECIALLY TRUE WITH
CHILDREN; IF YOU SEE ONE
WITH A PAINT POT, IT'S
BEST NOT TO SAY, "DO **NOT**
PAINT ON THE WALL." THE
CHILD HEARS "DO NOT
PAINT ON THE WALL!"
RESULTS GUARANTEED!!!

ANOTHER PLACE WE SLIP IS THE SLIPPERY

SYLLOGISM.

YOU REMEMBER THE SYLLOGISM?

"ALL MEN ARE MORTAL.
SOCRATES IS A MAN.
THEREFORE,
SOCRATES IS MORTAL."

SIMPLE, EH? TWO PREMISES AND A CONCLUSION... THAT'S HOW WE THINK, ISN'T IT?

AS SIMPLE AS FALLING OFF A LOG...

IT TURNS OUT THAT WE ARE FAIRLY TALENTED AT SOLVING SYLLOGISMS, AT LEAST SOME SYLLOGISMS... BUT WHEN THE PREMISES BEGIN TO DEPART FROM REALITY, THEN CONFUSION SETS IN... FOR INSTANCE...

ALL MBA'S ARE MORTAL. SOCRATES IS AN MBA... THEREFORE...

SOCRATES IS AN M.B.A.?

SOME CHAIRS ARE ERGONOMIC.
NO JUNK BOND IS ERGONOMIC.

THEREFORE...?

CONSIDER THIS SYLLOGISM...

PSYCHOLOGICAL STUDIES HAVE SHOWN THAT AROUND **HALF** OF ANY RANDOMLY CHOSEN GROUP OF PEOPLE CAN DRAW NO VALID CONCLUSION FROM SUCH PREMISES — AND YET FORMAL LOGIC SAYS THERE IS ONE. CAN YOU TELL WHAT IT IS?

DON'T SELL CHAIRS AND BONDS IN THE SAME STORE?

CLOSE... HOW ABOUT "SOME CHAIRS ARE NOT JUNK BONDS?"

YOU AREN'T SURE? TRY THIS ONE:

SOME BIRDS CAN SWIM.
NO FISH ARE BIRDS.
THEREFORE, SOME SWIMMERS ARE NOT FISH.

IN THIS CASE, THE CONCLUSION FEELS RIGHT. APPARENTLY, OUR LOGICAL ABILITIES IMPROVE WHEN WE CAN FIND SIMPLE MEANINGS IN THE SYLLOGISM!

ALL DUCKS ARE LUCKY CLUCKS. NO DUCK IS A TRUCK. THEREFORE, SOME LUCKY CLUCKS ARE NOT TRUCKS.

DO YOU KNOW ANY ABOUT STARFISH?

IT SEEMS THAT WE HAVE TROUBLE REASONING LOGICALLY WHEN CONFRONTED WITH UNFAMILIAR CONCEPTS. UNFORTUNATELY, THAT IS THE TIME WHEN WE ARE MOST IN NEED OF RATIONAL THOUGHT!!

GLASNOST

EUROPEAN UNIFICATION

SATELLITE WARFARE

ISLAMIC FUNDAMENT-ALISM

HERE'S A MAJOR SOURCE OF CONFUSION: WE DON'T COPE VERY WELL WITH CHANGE! LANGUAGE IS BASED ON EXPERIENCE, AND WHERE THERE IS NO EXPERIENCE, OUR MINDS HAVE A PROBLEM REMAINING RATIONAL.

SZRELTY?

EE HEE HEE E E

HOW CAN PEOPLE GET COMFORTABLE WITH NOVELTY? AGAIN WE TURN TO THE ANCIENT SPARTANS, AND THEIR LAWS, FOR ONE ANSWER...

HEY, WHAT'S ANCIENT?

OH, EVERYTHING. WHAT'S ANCIENT WITH YOU?

LEGEND HAS IT THAT THE SPARTAN LAWGIVER **LYKOURGOS** GOT SPARTA'S LAWS DIRECTLY FROM THE ORACLE AT DELPHI, MOUTHPIECE OF A GOD...

LYKOURGOS KNEW HOW HARD IT WAS FOR PEOPLE TO SWALLOW ANYTHING NEW. HE THOUGHT IT WOULD HELP MOTIVATE FOLKS IF THEY THOUGHT HIS LAWS WERE **DIVINELY INSPIRED!**

WOW!

GOSH!

WHEW!

WORKED FOR ME, TOO!

60

GOOD NEWS, PERKINS — YOUR TERMINATION IS DIVINELY INSPIRED.

EVEN WHEN WE THINK ABOUT FAMILIAR IDEAS, WE CAN LOSE OUR LOGICAL ABILITY. WE TEND TO DISMISS VALID CONCLUSIONS IF THEY CONFLICT WITH OUR BELIEFS — AND WELCOME INVALID BUT COMFORTABLE LOGIC! FOR INSTANCE:

"DEMOCRATS BELIEVE IN FREE SPEECH.
FASCISTS ARE NOT DEMOCRATS.
THEREFORE, FASCISTS DO NOT BELIEVE
    IN FREE SPEECH."
        (INVALID)

"WHATEVER CAUSES FULL EMPLOYMENT IS GOOD FOR SOCIETY.
WAR CAUSES FULL EMPLOYMENT.
THEREFORE, WAR IS GOOD FOR SOCIETY."
        (VALID.)

WE HAVE A MECHANISM FOR REJECTING DISAGREEABLE THOUGHTS!

... WAR IS GO

ONE MAY DEPLORE OUR EAGERNESS TO AVOID UNPLEASANT BUT VALID CONCLUSIONS. WHY DO WE DO THAT?

BECAUSE YOU AREN'T COMPUTERS. POOR THINGS.

WE DO IT BECAUSE WE ALWAYS INSTINCTIVELY NOTICE **MEANING.** INSTEAD OF CONCENTRATING ON THE LOGICAL STRUCTURE, WE LOOK BEHIND IT AT THE REAL-WORLD REFERENCES CONTAINED IN THE PREMISES.

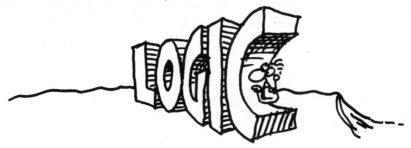

FOR EXAMPLE, NO ONE HAS EVER SEEN A FASCIST WHO BELIEVES IN FREE SPEECH... INDEED, FREE SPEECH AND FASCISM SEEM INCOMPATIBLE... SO, IN ACCEPTING THE SYLLOGISM ON THE PREVIOUS PAGE, WE HAVE MEASURED THE CONCLUSION AGAINST MORE THAN THE PREMISES: WE HAVE MEASURED IT AGAINST THE REAL WORLD.

"I MAY NOT AGREE WITH WHAT YOU SAY, BUT I WILL DEFEND TO THE DEATH YOUR RIGHT TO SAY IT..."

WELCOME TO WONDERLAND

HOW, THEN, DOES ANYONE COME TO THINK LOGICALLY??

TODAY, CLASS, WE CONSIDER WHETHER DUCKS ARE LUCKY CLUCKS...

THIS, IT TURNS OUT, IS LARGELY A MATTER OF EDUCATION. THE MORE SCHOOLING YOU HAVE, THE MORE COMFORTABLE YOU ARE LIKELY TO BE WITH ABSTRACT LOGICAL MANIPULATION OF THINGS OUTSIDE YOUR EXPERIENCE.

PSYCHOLOGISTS STUDYING UNSCHOOLED VILLAGERS FIND THEM TO BE "PRE-LOGICAL." THEIR REASONING IS SENSIBLE — BUT THEY REFUSE TO GO BEYOND THE HERE-AND-NOW. FOR EXAMPLE, A NIGERIAN FARMER IS ASKED: "ALL KPELLE GROW RICE. MR. SMITH DOES NOT GROW RICE. IS MR. SMITH A KPELLE?" THE ANSWER: "I DO NOT KNOW THE MAN." CONCLUSION?

YOU ARE "PRE-LOGICAL." POOR CHAP.

HM. AND YOU ARE STANDING IN QUICKSAND.

BY NOW, YOU PROBABLY AGREE THAT LANGUAGE IS NOT ENTIRELY LOGICAL, TO PUT IT MILDLY...

LANGUAGE IS EVIL!

MISLEADING

I'M GOING TO STOP USING IT!

IN THE SEVENTEENTH CENTURY, THE PHILOSOPHER LEIBNIZ IMAGINED THAT LOGIC WOULD SAVE THE WORLD... CONVERSATION WOULD BE AUTOMATIC... JUSTICE WOULD BE DISPENSED BY A MACHINE...

IT LOOKS AS IF THE PHILOSOPHER'S DREAM WAS A HALLUCINATION...

EVEN IF WE COULD DRAW PERFECT CONCLUSIONS, WE WOULD STILL BE IN TROUBLE... THERE IS NO AGREEMENT ON FIRST PRINCIPLES... WHERE PEOPLE AGREE ON FIRST PRINCIPLES, THEY WILL FIGHT OVER SECOND PRINCIPLES, ETC....

ALLAH IS GREAT ...

DON'T GET ME STARTED!!

64

SO LANGUAGE IS NOT ALWAYS LOGICAL... BUT THIS SHOULDN'T SURPRISE ANYONE!! LANGUAGE DOES MORE THAN ACT AS A MEDIUM FOR LOGICAL REASONING. IT ALSO... IT... IT... WHAT EXACTLY **DOES** LANGUAGE DO ???

IN PRINTED FORM, IT MAKES AN EXCELLENT DOOR STOP!

THE LINGUIST **ROMAN JAKOBSON,** WHO THOUGHT ABOUT THIS QUESTION FOR AT LEAST TEN MINUTES, CAME UP WITH A CLASSIFICATION THAT HAS BEEN WIDELY CITED.

ACCORDING TO JAKOBSON'S SCHEME, THERE ARE JUST **SIX** KINDS OF LINGUISTIC EXPRESSION. THESE ARE, IN HIS WORDS:

EMOTIVE
CONATIVE
REFERENTIAL
PHATIC
POETIC
METALINGUISTIC

AI, ROMAN! SUCH WORDS!

PARENTHETICALLY, BEFORE LOOKING AT JAKOBSON'S MEANING, JUST LOOK AT HIS WORDS! WHY IS IT THAT SCIENTISTS (AND QUASI-SCIENTISTS) LOVE THESE MASSIVE GRECO-ROMAN TERMINOLOGIES??

OLD LANGUAGES FOR NEW IDEAS?

YOU KNOW WHY... THE TECHNICAL JARGON MAINTAINS THE CULT STATUS OF SCIENCE, REASSURING SCIENTISTS AND STRIKING AWE INTO THE HEARTS OF OUTSIDERS...)

KROWOWAFGI?
SEMEMEMI !!
SEIKRONTO PRAFIPLO.
BIFZI, BAFZI;
HULALOMI...
QUASTI BESTI BO... *

* FROM DER GROSSE LALULA, BY C. MORGENSTERN.

67

SO...WITH MY HEARTFELT APOLOGIES FOR HIS TERMINOLOGY, HERE IS AN EXPLANATION OF MR. JAKOBSEN'S SIX FUNCTIONS OF LANGUAGE:

EMOTIVE:

THIS REFERS TO UTTERANCES THAT EXPRESS EMOTION—EXPRESS, NOT DESCRIBE—SUCH AS:

CONATIVE

EXPRESSIONS SEEK TO PRODUCE BEHAVIOR.

COME HITHER.   GET STUFFED.

PHATIC

EXPRESSIONS ARE VERBAL FEEDBACK THAT SIGNAL SOMEONE THAT YOU ARE LISTENING.

BLAH BLAH BLAH BLAH BLAH BLAH BLAH BLAH BLAH BLAH...

YEH... GRUNT... UM... EH?

POETIC:

HERE MEANING IS SECONDARY, AND THE QUALITY, SOUND, OR TEXTURE OF LANGUAGE ITSELF CAME FIRST.

IN THE JINGLE-JANGLE MORNING I'LL COME FOLLOWING YEW...

REFERENTIAL:

THIS IS THE ONE YOU WOULD PROBABLY THINK OF FIRST. REFERENTIAL SENTENCES REFER TO THE OUTSIDE (OR INSIDE) WORLD.

THIS IS A HOUSE.

METALINGUISTIC:

LANGUAGE TALKING ABOUT LANGUAGE.

THIS SENTENCE IS FALSE.

PHAT

WE WANT TO MAKE TWO POINTS ABOUT THIS SCHEME, WHICH WILL BRING US BACK TO WHERE WE BEGAN...

 THESE CATEGORIES ARE RATHER FLUID... THEY HAVE FUZZY EDGES. MANY SENTENCES FALL UNDER TWO OR MORE HEADINGS AT ONCE. LANGUAGE IS WONDERFULLY FLEXIBLE, WITH MULTIPLE MEANINGS.

A **PHATIC** EXPRESSION, FOR EXAMPLE, MAY ALSO BE EMOTIVE AND EVEN CONATIVE, ALL AT THE SAME TIME.

A PHATIC STATEMENT

BLAH BLAH TALK TALK NATTER NATTER

REALLY?

TAKEN AS EMOTIVE

YOU SOUND SKEPTICAL!

MAY STIMULATE ACTION!

HERE. THIS 1000-PAGE BOOK WILL PROVE MY POINT...

SIMILARLY, **POETIC** LANGUAGE IS SUPPOSED TO SOUND MUSICAL, BUT IT CAN ALSO HAVE OTHER FUNCTIONS.

ADVERTISING IS POETIC (IN ITS WAY!), BUT IT ALSO REFERS TO A PRODUCT AND URGES US TO TAKE ACTION AND BUY. IMAGINE ADVERTISING WITHOUT POETRY...

WITHOUT POETRY: "BUY THIS PRODUCT. IT IS ABOUT AS GOOD AS MOST OF THE OTHER BRANDS. YOU WILL PROBABLY LIKE IT AT FIRST, AND WE NEED THE MONEY."

WITH: "TOUCH THE POWER. FEEL THE PASSION... EXPERIENCE THE PERFORMANCE OF SLEEK AUTO-MOBILES MODELED BY WOMEN PRETENDING TO FLIRT WITH YOU..."

2. DESPITE THEIR COLD, "OBJECTIVE" SOUND, MOST OF JAKOBSON'S CATEGORIES ARE CLOSELY ASSOCIATED WITH OUR *Emotional life!* (YES, THERE WE ARE AGAIN!)

WITH **EMOTIVE** STATEMENTS, IT'S OBVIOUS: THEY EXPRESS RAW EMOTION!

WHEE!

WHAT ABOUT **CONATIVE** STATEMENTS? THEY ARE SUPPOSED TO INDUCE ACTION— AND WHAT STIMULATES ACTION BETTER THAN EMOTIONS LIKE DESIRE AND FEAR?

IF YOU FILE YOUR REPORT PROMPTLY, YOU WILL RECEIVE A PROMOTION AND A BONUS, WHEREAS IF IT COMES IN AFTER TUESDAY, I SHALL HAVE TO APPLY THIS ELECTRIC CATTLE PROD TO YOUR ENTIRE DEPARTMENT. NOW MOVE.

EEK!

EVEN OUR **PHATIC** GRUNTS SERVE AN EMOTIONAL PURPOSE: BY MAINTAINING CONTACT, THEY OFFER COMFORT AND REASSURANCE.

AND THEN I...

YUP... UH HUH... SURE...

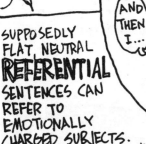

OF COURSE, **POETRY** IS THE LANGUAGE OF EMOTION...

SUPPOSEDLY FLAT, NEUTRAL **REFERENTIAL** SENTENCES CAN REFER TO EMOTIONALLY CHARGED SUBJECTS.

HICKORY DICKORY DOCK. THE MOUSE RAN UP THE CLOCK...

IN OTHER NEWS, THE HBN CORPORATION ANNOUNCED THE IMMEDIATE TERMINATION OF EVERYONE WATCHING THIS BROADCAST...

ONLY METALINGUISTIC TALK IS COMPLETELY UNEMOTIONAL — UNLESS YOU HAPPEN TO BE A LINGUIST.

BIFZI, BAFZI

· CHAPTER 5 ·
CLEARLY!

AMELIORATING OBFUSCATION NECESSITATES OPTIMIZING
ADHERENCE TO A TETRADIC DECOMPLEXIFICATION SCHEMA.

OF ALL THE EMOTIONS WE FEEL IN THE PRESENCE OF LANGUAGE, SURELY FEW CAN COMPARE WITH THE PLEASURE, THE GRATITUDE, THE RELIEF, THE INNER HARMONY WE FEEL WHEN WE HEAR A MESSAGE EXPRESSED WITH BEAUTIFUL CLARITY.

EVEN VERY UNPLEASANT MESSAGES CAN BE STRANGELY SATISFYING, IF THEY ARE DELIVERED IN SIMPLE LANGUAGE. AT LEAST THE MEANING IS NOT HIDDEN!

I SUPPOSE THIS FEELING COMES FROM THE FACT THAT SO MUCH COMMUNICATION TODAY IS CONFUSED, MANIPULATIVE, SELF-SERVING, AND OTHERWISE UNTRUSTWORTHY... FROM THE GIANT FALSEHOODS OF GOVERNMENT TO THE SMALLER SLOPPINESS OF CORPORATE MEMORANDA... SORRY IF I SOUND CYNICAL...

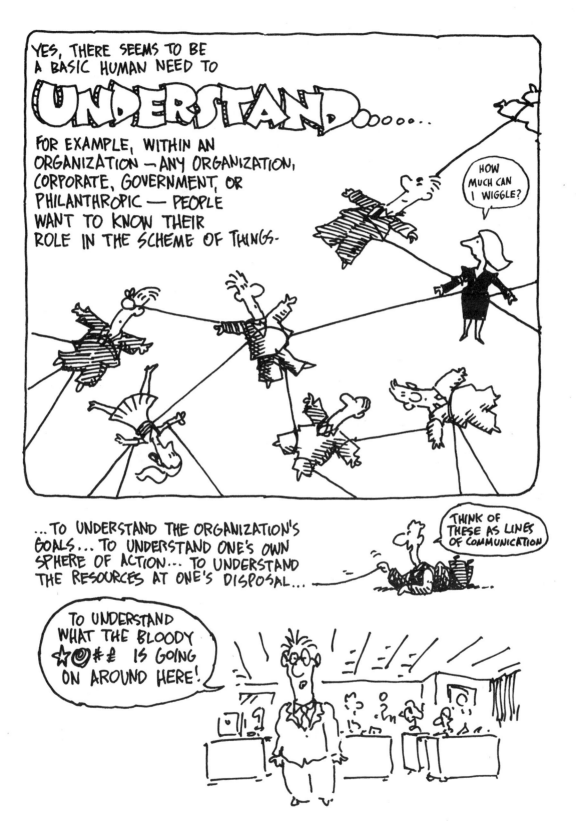

BY NOW, WE UNDERSTAND* THAT UNDERSTANDING IS RARELY 100% PERFECT. IF I SEND YOU A MESSAGE, I EXPRESS CONCEPTS FROM MY EXPERIENCE... AND YOU HEAR CONCEPTS BASED ON YOUR EXPERIENCE.

AND WE HOPE OUR CONCEPT BALLOONS OVERLAP!

*IMPERFECTLY, TO BE SURE!

(ACCORDING TO ONE THEORY, BY THE WAY, **GESTURES** ARE NOTHING BUT ATTEMPTS TO POINT AT OR DESCRIBE THE STUFF IN YOUR [INVISIBLE] CONCEPT CLOUD. MAKES SENSE!)

AND ANOTHER PROBLEM, NOTED BY THE SUBTLE PHILOSOPHER WILLARD VAN ORMAN **QUINE:** WE ALWAYS OVERESTIMATE THE DEGREE TO WHICH WE ARE UNDERSTOOD!

BLAH BLAH BLAH BLAH BLAH BLAH BLAH

THAT IS, WHEN I TALK, I ASSUME YOU UNDERSTAND ME—UNLESS YOU TELL ME OTHERWISE!

AND THERE ARE A LOT OF REASONS YOU MAY NOT GIVE ME THIS ESSENTIAL FEEDBACK:

* YOU'RE TOO POLITE

* YOU THOUGHT YOU GOT IT, EVEN THOUGH YOU DIDN'T

* YOU'RE AFRAID OF LOOKING STUPID

SO, WE AGREE?

I MUST BE SLOW.

THE RESULT IS A WORLDWIDE OVERVALUATION OF THE LEVEL OF UNDERSTANDING !!!

WITH ALL DUE MODESTY, THEN, HERE ARE FOUR TENTATIVE PRINCIPLES OF CLEAR COMMUNICATION:

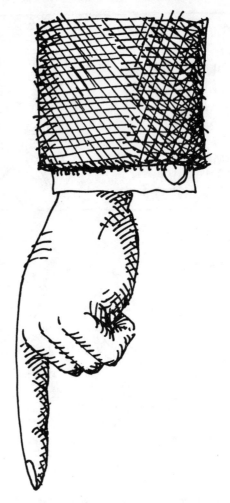

NECESSARY BUT NOT SUFFICIENT!

1. UNDERSTAND YOUR MESSAGE BEFORE YOU SEND IT.

2. SPEAK THE "OTHER GUY'S LANGUAGE."

3. KEEP IT SIMPLE.

4. INVITE FEEDBACK.

1. UNDERSTAND

YOUR OWN MESSAGE BEFORE YOU SEND IT...

YOU AGAIN?

THIS IS A MATTER OF CONFRONTING YOUR "INNER REPTILE..." OF EXAMINING YOUR OWN ASSUMPTIONS AND DESIRES... ASSESSING YOUR EMOTIONAL INVESTMENT IN THE MESSAGE... QUESTIONING YOUR OWN LOGIC... AND DECIDING WHETHER WHAT YOU ARE SAYING REALLY MAKES SENSE, OR IF YOU ONLY <u>HOPE</u> IT MAKES SENSE.

2. SPEAK

THE "OTHER GUY'S LANGUAGE:" THIS GOES BACK TO THE STORY OF "TWO GUYS, ONE STICK." IT REQUIRES SOME UNDERSTANDING OF HOW THE RECIPIENT OF YOUR MESSAGE HAS EXPERIENCED THE WORLD, AND A RECOGNITION THAT DIFFERENT WORDS MEAN DIFFERENT THINGS TO DIFFERENT PEOPLE— AND SOME WORDS CAN MEAN ALMOST NOTHING AT ALL!

KROKOWAFGI THE HULAGOMI. HAVE IT BY TWO O'CLOCK.

GAH!

3. KEEP IT SIMPLE!

IT'S SURPRISINGLY DIFFICULT TO SAY
EXACTLY WHAT THIS MEANS. AT THE
VERY LEAST, IT INVOLVES USING
KINESTHETIC AND VISUAL LANGUAGE
WHENEVER POSSIBLE... BUT, IN GENERAL,
SIMPLIFICATION IS THE HARDEST THING:
A REAL ART!!

4. INVITE FEEDBACK!

WE ALL WANT PEOPLE TO AGREE WITH US — EVEN MORE THAN WE
WANT THEM TO UNDERSTAND US. THIS MAKES IT HARD TO HEAR
THEIR NEGATIVE FEEDBACK. BUT CLEAR COMMUNICATION REQUIRES
FEEDBACK! OTHERWISE, HOW DO YOU KNOW IT WAS CLEAR???

80

TO APPRECIATE CLEAR COMMUNICATION, IT MIGHT HELP TO LOOK AT SOME UNCLEAR EXAMPLES, LITTERED WITH BROKEN RULES:

AN EXAMPLE OF FAILING TO FOLLOW RULE No. 1 IS THE CORPORATE STRATEGIC PLAN. EVERYONE KNOWS THAT NO ONE READS IT... UNDER THE CIRCUMSTANCES, HOW CAN A MANAGER EXPLAIN CORPORATE GOALS TO HIS OR HER SUBORDINATES? IT'S LIKE A GAME OF TELEPHONE!

WE SEEK A 20% INCREASE IN GROSS REVENUE NEXT YEAR.

WE SEEK GROSS INCREASES IN REVENUE NEXT YEAR.

NEXT YEAR, WE HOPE TO GET MUCH GROSSER.

NEXT YEAR WE ACQUIRE A GROCERY.

BUY MILK!

MANAGEMENT GURU TOM "EXCELLENCE" PETERS SUGGESTS LIMITING THE STRATEGIC PLAN TO A SINGLE PAGE, WHICH ANYONE COULD READ, REMEMBER, AND EXPLAIN IN A FEW MINUTES!

DIGEST THE PLAN YET?

I'M CHEWING ON IT...

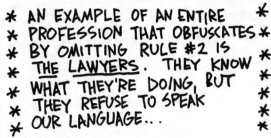

* AN EXAMPLE OF AN ENTIRE
* PROFESSION THAT OBFUSCATES
* BY OMITTING RULE #2 IS
* THE <u>LAWYERS</u>. THEY KNOW
* WHAT THEY'RE DOING, BUT
* THEY REFUSE TO SPEAK
* OUR LANGUAGE...

OBITER DICTA

HABEUS CORPUS

NON COMPOS MENTIS

PRO BONO   IPSO FACTO

I THINK THEY LEARN TO DO THIS IN SECRET RITUALS LED BY SPARTAN LAW SCHOOL PROFESSORS.

AND A CASE OF VIOLATING RULE #3 WHILE OBSERVING #1 AND #2 WOULD BE...AT LEAST IN MY COUNTRY... THE **INCOME TAX FORMS.**

THE AUTHORS PROBABLY KNOW WHAT THEY MEAN ... THE FORMS **SEEM** TO MAKE SENSE ... BUT SIMPLE ?

PHEW
!!
oo

I CAN'T LOOK!

4868

Form Department of the Treasury Internal Revenue Service (I)

General Instructions

Paperwork Reduction Act Notice.— We ask for this information to carry out the Internal Revenue laws of the United States. We need it to ensure that taxpayers are complying with these laws and to allow us to figure and collect the right amount of tax. You are required to give us this information.

The time needed to complete and file this form will vary depending on individual circumstances. The estimated average time is: **Recordkeeping**, 26 minutes; **Learning about the law or the form**, 11 minutes; and **Preparing the form**, 18 minutes; and **Copying, assembling, and sending the form to IRS**, 20 minutes.

If you have comments concerning the accuracy of these time estimates or suggestions for making this form more simple, we would be happy to hear from you. You can write to the Internal Revenue Service, Washington, DC 20224, Attention:

Application to...
To File U.S. Individ...

IRS Reports Clearance Officer, TR:r... the **Office of Management and Budget,** Paperwork Reduction Project, Washington, DC 20503.

Purpose

Use Form 4868 to ask for 4 more months to file **Form 1040A or Form 1040**. You do not have to give a reason why you are asking for the extension.

To get the extra time you **MUST:**
1. Fill in Form 4868 correctly, **AND**
2. File it by the due date of your return, A...
3. Pay ALL of the tax shown on line 6.
We will contact you only if your requ... denied.

If you already had 2 extra months because you were "out of the count... page 2) when your return was due... can only get 2 more months using...

Do not file Form 4868 if you w... figure your tax, or are under a c... file your return by the regular...

NOW FOR A COUPLE OF FINE EXAMPLES OF CLARITY: IN SOME PARTS OF THE U.S.A., WE HAVE A MOVEMENT TOWARD

PLAIN ENGLISH CONTRACTS, TAX FORMS, GAS AND ELECTRIC BILLS, ETC... LAWYERS AND LATIN TEACHERS, BEWARE!!

GLEEP!

A LOAN AGREEMENT WRITTEN BY SIMPLIFICATION EXPERTS **SIEGEL & GALE** REPLACES

THIS:

"In the event of default of the payment of this or any other obligation or the performance or observance of any term or covenant contained herein or in any note or other contract or agreement evidencing or relating to any obligation or any collateral on the borrower's part to be performed or observed; or the...[many more lines]... then the bank shall have the right (at its option) without demand or notice of any kind, to declare all or any part of the obligations to be immediately due and payable, whereupon..."

WITH THIS:

Default: I'll be in default
   1. If I don't pay an installment on time

or   2. If any other creditor tries by legal process to take any money of mine in your possession

   You may then demand immediate payment of the balance of this note...

AMONG ITS OTHER MERITS, THE NEW VERSION ELIMINATES ENORMOUS NUMBERS OF SPECIALIZED TERMS: OUT GO "OBLIGATION", "PERFORMANCE", "OBSERVANCE", "COVENANT", "HEREIN", "EVIDENCING", "COLLATERAL", "OPTION" .... ETC.

HELP! COUGH! FIRE!

IT REPLACES THEM WITH VIVID, CONCRETE, EVEN KINESTHETIC LANGUAGE!

BZZ BZZ DON'T PAY BZZ BZZ TAKE ANY MONEY OF MINE BZZ BZZ

I WISH CONTRACTS HAD LOOKED LIKE THIS IN MY DAY...

IT IS ALSO CLEAR THAT THE LANGUAGE OF THE CONTRACT HAS BEEN **SIMPLIFIED.** INDEED, ITS AUTHORS SIEGEL & GALE HAVE THE MOTTO "SMART IS SIMPLE." BUT WHAT DOES IT MEAN, TO SIMPLIFY? ISN'T IT OBVIOUS THAT **BAD** SIMPLIFICATION, OR **OVER**SIMPLIFICATION, IS NOT SMART, BUT STUPID??

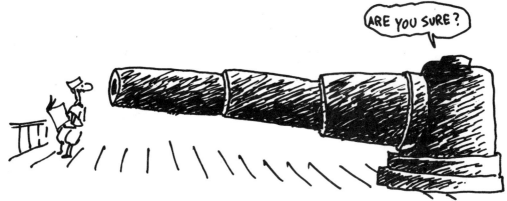

SO, WHAT IS SIMPLIFICATION? DOES IT MEAN PENETRATING TO THE ESSENTIAL CORE OF INFORMATION? UNDERSTANDING ITS LOGIC? DISCARDING INESSENTIALS? REARRANGEMENT? DOES IT HAVE A VISUAL DIMENSION? DOES IT INVOLVE TRIAL·AND·ERROR? IS IT A SUBTLE ART?

TO SEE THAT SIMPLIFICATION MEANS MORE THAN JUST MAKING SOMETHING LOGICAL, NOTE THAT THE **LOGIC** OF THE DEFAULT CLAUSE IS:

IF THE BORROWER IS IN DEFAULT, **OR** ETC ETC ETC... **THEN** THE BANK MAY BLAH BLAH BLAH **UNLESS** IT CHOOSES NOT TO... ETC ETC...

ACTUALLY CLOSER TO THE ORIGINAL VERSION...

THE "LEGALESE" IS, IN FACT, STRICTLY LOGICAL !!!

BUT THE HUMAN (AS OPPOSED TO THE LEGAL) MIND HAS TROUBLE FOLLOWING A LOGICAL STRUCTURE IF THE TERMS ARE STRANGE OR UNFAMILIAR. ONLY A LAWYER OR A LOGICIAN COULD READ THAT CONTRACT!

I GET IT! $D \lor Q_1 \lor Q_2 \lor Q_3 \rightarrow B \land \sim A_1 \ldots$

GAH!

FOR MOST OF US, THE NATURAL, HUMAN IMPULSE IS TO ASK QUESTIONS....
AND IF "SIMPLIFICATION" MEANS ANYTHING, IT MEANS ANSWERING THE READER'S QUESTIONS IN THE ORDER THEY COME UP!!

WHAT THE —? WHAT **IS** DEFAULT? WHAT ARE THEY TRYING TO **DO** TO ME? ETC ETC

ONLY ONE THING TO DO: RUN!

THIS MAKES SIMPLIFICATION AN EXAMPLE
OF "ERGONOMICS—

DESIGN WITH HUMAN NEEDS
IN MIND. ERGONOMICS USUALLY
REFERS TO PHYSICAL NEEDS—
ERGONOMIC FURNITURE FOR YOUR
BACK, ERGONOMIC LIGHTING
FOR YOUR EYES, ERGONOMIC
TELEPHONES FOR YOUR NECK—
BUT THERE MUST ALSO BE AN
ERGONOMICS OF THE MIND!

NOTE:
ERGONOMICS
WAS NOT EVEN
A WORD IN
1971!

HEAD PHONES

OVER LEFT SHOULDER

BACK SUPPORT

* *

ANOTHER EXAMPLE OF "MENTAL ERGONOMICS" IS THE

✳MACINTOSH COMPUTER✳

(AND ITS COUSINS!)

ME AGAIN!

THE EVOLUTION OF
SOFTWARE AND THE
MACHINE-USER INTERFACE
IS A GRADUAL
DEVELOPMENT TOWARDS
"USER-FRIENDLY"
SYSTEMS.

IN OLDEN TIMES (SAY, 1953) THE COMPUTER LIVED IN ITS OWN TEMPLE, THE "COMPUTER CENTER," ATTENDED BY A SPECIALIZED PRIESTHOOD OF TECHNICIANS WHO UNDERSTOOD THE MYSTERIES OF PUNCH CARDS, BATCH PROCESSING, AND CORE MEMORIES. NOWADAYS WE WOULD THINK OF THESE RUMPLED INDIVIDUALS AS "COMPUTER FRIENDLY."

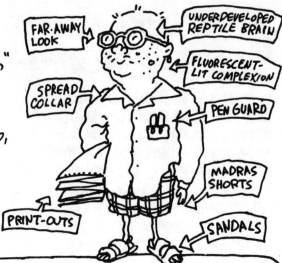

THEN THE MICROCOMPUTER REVOLUTION BROUGHT THE MACHINE OUT OF THE SACRED PRECINCT AND INTO THE USER'S LAP —

FOLLOWED DIRECTLY BY AN EMOTIONAL REACTION CALLED COMPUTERPHOBIA. THESE GADGETS MADE PEOPLE NERVOUS! AND RIGHTLY SO...

THE EARLY MICROCOMPUTERS HAD AN INHUMAN FACE. THE USER HAD TO PRACTICE STRANGE AND DIFFICULT RITUALS, SUCH AS MEMORIZING MANUALS FULL OF UNINTUITIVE COMMANDS.

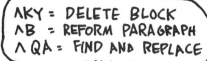

^KY = DELETE BLOCK
^B = REFORM PARAGRAPH
^QA = FIND AND REPLACE

^KE = RENAME FILE, ^KK = END OF BLOCK... ETC

(LEARNING WORDSTAR WAS A LITTLE LIKE CHANTING THE SPARTAN LAWS!

THEN, IN THE LATE '60'S, COMPUTER. JOCKEY **ALAN KAY** AND HIS FELLOW VISIONARIES AT THE XEROX PALO ALTO RESEARCH CENTER INVENTED A LANGUAGE CALLED SMALLTALK.

THE SMALLTALK LANGUAGE WAS DESIGNED TO ENABLE CHILDREN TO USE THE COMPUTER. IMMEDIATELY, JEROME BRUNER'S IDEAS CAME INTO PLAY...

FROM THESE EXPERIMENTS CAME MANY NEW IDEAS OF USER-FRIENDLINESS, WHICH EVOLVED INTO THE GRAPHIC USER INTERFACES (GUIs) OF TODAY.

NOTE HOW A GOOD GUI FOLLOWS OUR FOUR RULES:

1. THE DESIGNERS KNEW WHAT THEY WERE TRYING TO DO.

2. THEY REPRESENTED DATA STRUCTURES WITH ICONS AND LANGUAGE FAMILIAR TO ALL: "FOLDERS," NOT "DIRECTORIES," ETC.

3. THEY ARRANGED THE SCREEN IN AN ORDERLY, CLEAR, AND CONSISTENT WAY!

4. THEY OFFERED THE USER SOUND AND GRAPHIC FEEDBACK: FOLDERS THAT APPEAR TO OPEN, "DIALOG BOXES," ETC.

THE WONDERFUL THING ABOUT THESE "POINT-AND-CLICK" MACHINES IS HOW **APPROACHABLE** THEY ARE. THE (SOMEWHAT) SELF-EXPLANATORY ICONS INVITE YOU TO BEGIN USING THE COMPUTER IMMEDIATELY, WITHOUT FIRST MEMORIZING AN ENORMOUS MANUAL. LIKE THE PLAIN-ENGLISH LOAN AGREEMENT, THE MACINTOSH ANSWERS YOUR QUESTIONS WHEN YOU ASK THEM!

AS WE ALL KNOW, POINTING AND CLICKING IS NOT THE MOST NATURAL FORM OF HUMAN COMMUNICATION. WHAT, WE MAY WONDER, WILL THE ULTIMATE COMPUTER BE LIKE?

TALKING COMPUTERS MAY ARRIVE SOON, BUT THEY AREN'T READY YET!

YOU REALLY ARE STUPID AND USELESS!

THANK YOU—SKWEET

HAIRY COMPUTERS MIGHT ADD A WARM, COMFORTABLE, DOG-LIKE FEELING.

IT'S SHEDDING.

SEXY ANDROIDS WOULD STIMULATE USER INTEREST, THOUGH IT MIGHT PROVE DISTRACTING.

HELLO, SALLY! WOULD-YOU-LIKE-TO COMMUNICATE-WITH-ME? FIRST-TRY-TO FIND-MY-MOUSE-HA-HA-HA!

HOW ABOUT AN ANIMATED FACE OF YOUR CHOICE ON THE SCREEN?

HI THERE!

COMPUTERS THAT MANIPULATE **YOU**?

GET A MOUSE, JACK!

HOLOGRAPHIC, 3-D, "SENSURROUND" TOTAL ENVIRONMENTAL SIMU-LATORS INDISTINGUISHABLE FROM THE REAL WORLD? ONLY **BETTER**?

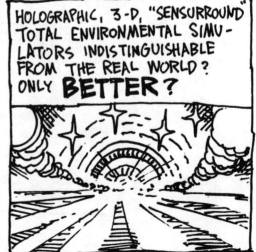

CHAPTER 6
◆ CHANGES ◆

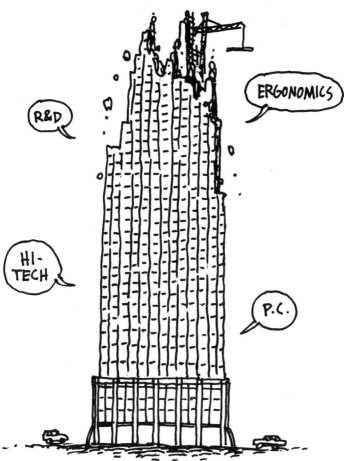

THE BABEL CONSTRUCTION COMPANY
HAS HIRED SOME NEW ARCHITECTS.

IN ANCIENT TIMES, WORDS WERE THOUGHT TO CARRY A MYSTIC POTENCY. TO NAME WAS TO GAIN POWER... FOR THIS REASON, THE ANCIENT HEBREWS AVOIDED EVER SPEAKING THE NAME OF GOD: THE SPEAKER WOULD DEVELOP GODLIKE POWERS!!

SHUT UP!

PARADOXICALLY, FOR THE VERY SAME REASON, SOME HINDUS CHANT THE NAME OF GOD CONTINUOUSLY!!!

POP   SNEP

HARI KRISHNA HARI RAMA KRISHNA KRISHNA
HARI HARI HARI RAMA RAMA RAMA HARI
RAMA KRISHNA KRISHNA KRISHNA
HARI HARI HARI KRISHNA HARI
KRISHNA HARI RAMA HARI
KRISHNA KRISHNA
KRISHNA RAMA
RAMA HARI
HARI...
(WHEW!)

TODAY, SOMETHING OF THIS ATTITUDE REMAINS: LANGUAGE IS DEVELOPING TO HELP US "GET A HANDLE" ON A WORLD GALLOPING INTO THE FUTURE!

FOR EXAMPLE!

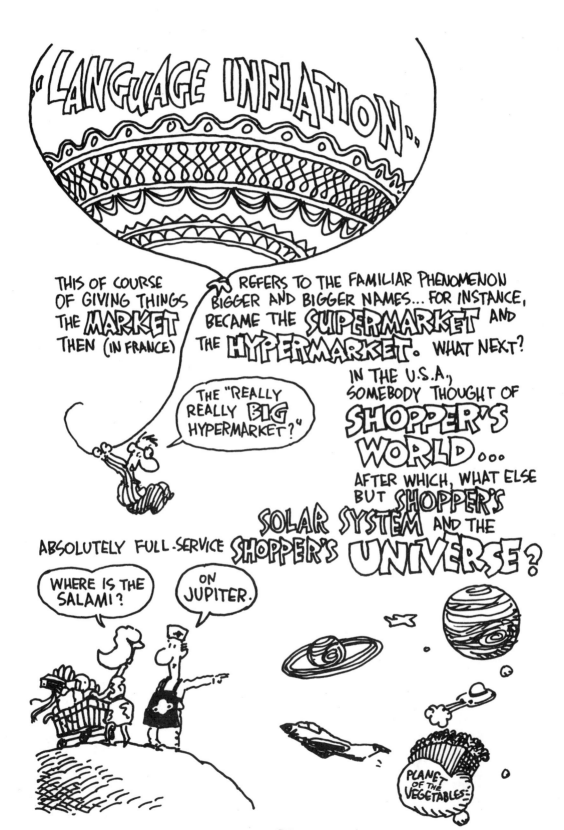

97

ONE RESULT OF THIS IS THAT SOME WORDS LOSE THEIR OLD MEANINGS.

THAT **IS** THE "LARGE" SIZE.

A FAMILIAR EXAMPLE IS TITLE-INFLATION. WHEN AN EMPLOYEE ASKS FOR A RAISE, IT'S EASIER TO GIVE A NEW TITLE, INSTEAD. (THIS IS AN EXAMPLE OF LANGUAGE TRYING TO SATISFY AN EMOTIONAL NEED.)

CONGRATULATIONS. A SWITCHBOARD OPERATOR NO LONGER, YOU ARE NOW VICE-PRESIDENT, CORPORATE COMMUNICATION.

IN AMERICA AT LEAST, THE TITLE OF "VICE PRESIDENT" HAS BECOME COMPLETELY DEBASED (IF IT EVER MEANT ANYTHING).

AND THIS IS OUR DEPARTMENT OF VICE-PRESIDENTS...

A LANGUAGE IS ALSO INFLATED BY "COINAGES," NEOLOGISMS, *NEW WORDS*... OR NEW COMBINATIONS THAT HAVE THE STATUS OF NEW WORDS.

INVENTING A WORD IS SOMETHING LIKE MAGIC: WHERE THERE HAD BEEN CONFUSION, SUDDENLY THERE IS MEANING! PRESTO!!

INFO DUC$

HERE, IN NO SPECIAL ORDER, ARE SOME OF THE WORDS THAT HAVE BUBBLED UP IN NEO-BABELONIA:

PC
WORKAHOLIC
BIOTECH
ERGONOMIC
EXPERT SYSTEM
STRATEGIC PLAN
FAX
downsizing
QUALITY CIRCLES
management by walking around
FutureShock
LEVERAGED BUY-OUT
RESEARCH AND DEVELOPMENT
MBA
CAD CAM
CHAOS
Information economy
Excellence
PAPERLESS SOCIETY
GROWTH
VENTURE CAPITAL
OFFICE AUTOMATION
GOAL-ORIENTED
GRAPHIC DESIGN
PRIVATE SECTOR
MARKET NICHE
intrapreneur
NEURO-LINGUISTING PROGRAMMER
CORPORATE CULTURE
TRANSACTIONAL ANALYSIS
LAPTOP
MEGA TRENDS
Paradigm

OUR VISIONARY FRIEND LUC DE BRABANDERE WONDERS, "WHY DO WE NEED ALL THIS NEW LANGUAGE? WHAT DOES IT ADD? IN THE OLD DAYS, THERE WAS A BOSS, A STAFF, AND WORK. WHY DO WE SUDDENLY HAVE HUMAN RESOURCES, ORGANIZATIONAL DEVELOPMENT, INFLUENCE WITH INTEGRITY, AND SYNERGY ???"

I SPRAINED MY TONGUE ON THAT LAST ONE...

I'LL BE HONEST. I DON'T KNOW THE ANSWER TO THAT QUESTION. IF YOU HAVE ANY IDEAS, SEND THEM TO YOUR CARTOONIST, c/o THE PUBLISHER, AND WE WILL INCLUDE YOUR SUGGESTIONS IN THE NEXT PRINTING...

IS IT A MATTER OF HOT TECHNOLOGY OR HOT AIR?

A FEW POSSIBILITIES:
TECHNOLOGY ALONE CREATES NEW WORDS IN HEAPS.

ORGANIZATIONS SEEK NEW STRUCTURES, LESS HIERARCHY.

PSYCHOLOFY AND THE HUMAN POTENTIAL MOVEMENT ENCOURAGE EVERYONE TO BE UNBLOCKED, ACTUALIZED, AUTONOMOUS!

IMAGE IS EVERYTHING.
OLD WORDS PROJECT AN IMPRESSION OF STAGNATION.

WHATEVER THE REASON, WE SEEM BOUND TO GO ON LIVING IN THIS NEO-BABELONIA. THE WORLD IS UNLIKELY TO STOP CHANGING!

AND LANGUAGE HAS NO "TOP FLOOR!"

ON THE PLUS SIDE, THE GLOBALIZATION OF ECONOMICS AND COMMUNICATION MAKES MANY OF THESE NEW ANGLO-GRECO-LATINISMS UNIVERSALLY UNDERSTOOD (WITH MINOR MODIFICATIONS).

OH, I SAY, "NLP..."

ET JE DIS, "PNL!"

FOR THE FORESEEABLE FUTURE, THE ONLY TRULY UNIVERSAL LANGUAGE WILL CONTINUE TO BE... BODY LANGUAGE!!

DON'T GO... THERE WAS NO MISTAKING THAT LOOK IN YOUR EYES...

PART TWO
· IMAGE ·

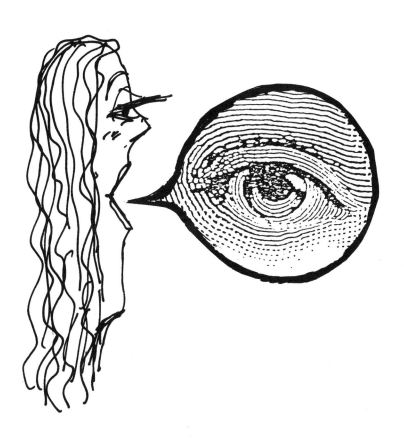

INTRODUCTION

TO PART TWO ....

STRANGE AS IT MAY SOUND, CREATING IMAGES IS LESS NATURAL THAN USING LANGUAGE. SPEECH IS A PART OF HUMAN BIOLOGY, INVOLVING NOTHING MORE THAN THE USE OF OUR BRAINS AND OUR TONGUES... BUT CREATING AN IMAGE REQUIRES

TECHNOLOGY.

WITHOUT TECHNOLOGY, THE ONLY IMAGE WE CAN PROJECT IS THE SIGHT OF OUR OWN BODIES, LIKE THE LOBSTERS IN CHAPTER 1.

BUT THANKS TO TECHNOLOGY, FROM THE FIRST CRAYON TO THE LATEST MULTIMEDIA MONSTER, HUMANITY HAS DEVELOPED THE ABILITY TO MAKE AND TRANSMIT IMAGES.

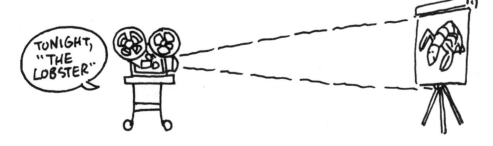

TONIGHT, "THE LOBSTER"

TODAY, WE'RE SO USED TO A ROUTINE BOMBARDMENT OF IMAGES, WE DON'T GIVE IT A SECOND THOUGHT.

THE DIGITAL REVOLUTION HAS COMBINED LANGUAGE AND IMAGE UNDER THE SINGLE HEADING OF "INFORMATION" (EVEN THOUGH WE RESPOND TO THEM IN VERY DIFFERENT WAYS). ALL COMMUNICATION IS BECOMING "INFORMATION PROCESSING."

IN THIS SECTION, WE'LL TRACE THE EVOLUTION OF IMAGE PROJECTION, FROM THE FIRST SCRIBBLE TO THE LATEST "SMART" TELEVISION, CONSIDER THE INTERPLAY OF WORDS AND PICTURES, AND LOOK AHEAD TO THE ONRUSHING DIGITAL MULTIMEDIA JUGGERNAUT WITH FEAR, TREMBLING, AND EVEN THE TINIEST TRACE OF OPTIMISM !!!

◊ CHAPTER 7 ◊
MAKING PICTURES, TAKING PICTURES

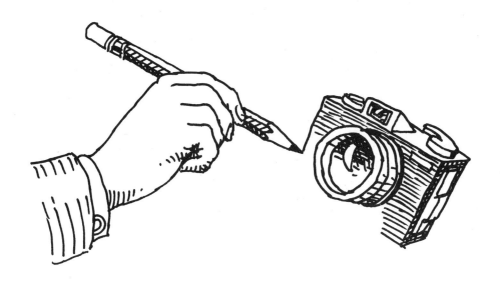

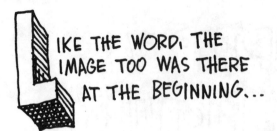

LIKE THE WORD, THE IMAGE TOO WAS THERE AT THE BEGINNING...

...BUT WITH A DIFFERENCE...

THE IMAGE, UNLIKE THE WORD, TRAVELED IN ONLY ONE DIRECTION. ALTHOUGH ANIMALS ARE EQUIPPED TO SEND AND RECEIVE SOUNDS, THEIR ABILITY TO SEND IMAGES IS ALL BUT NON-EXISTENT. EVERYONE HAS EYES, BUT NOBODY HAS A BUILT-IN IMAGE PROJECTOR!

TO BE MORE PRECISE — NO ANIMAL HAS AN **EXTERNAL** IMAGE-PROJECTOR. WE DO HAVE AN INTERNAL DEVICE FOR CREATING MENTAL IMAGES, WHICH CAN BE PROCESSED IN VARIOUS WAYS: ROTATION, ENLARGEMENT, BRIGHTNESS AND CONTRAST CONTROL, ETC.

THERE IS EXPERIMENTAL EVIDENCE THAT APES CAN DO THIS, TOO!

EVEN WITHOUT A PROJECTOR, VISUAL COMMUNICATION WAS STILL POSSIBLE... THROUGH "BODY LANGUAGE."

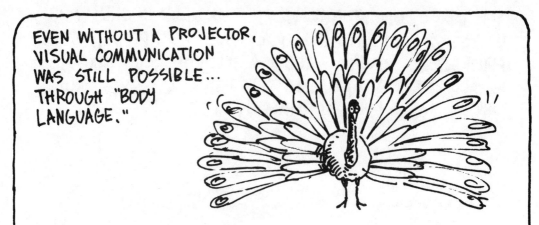

ANIMALS SEND VISUAL SIGNALS WITH GESTURES, POSES, ATTITUDES, FACIAL EXPRESSIONS. REMEMBER THOSE LOBSTERS IN CHAPTER ONE?

WELL, I'M STILL DOMINANT!

AMONG HUMANS, SOME BODY LANGUAGE, ESPECIALLY FACIAL EXPRESSION, GOES ALL THE WAY BACK TO THE APES. WE CAN "READ FACES" NO MATTER WHOSE THEY ARE!!

ANGRY HUMAN   ANGRY APE   ANGRY GRAPE

GESTURE AND POSTURE, TOO, ARE ASPECTS OF HUMAN BODY LANGUAGE...

TO WHICH WE ADDED THE EMBELLISHMENTS OF MAKE-UP, JEWELRY, HAIR STYLING, COSTUME, ETC.

WHAT ARE YOUR SHOULDERS TRYING TO SAY, GLORIA?

COSTUME, MAKE-UP, GESTURES, LANGUAGE, AND ALL CAME TOGETHER IN THEATER AND DANCE, WHICH YOU HAD TO BE THERE TO SEE.

LOW-TECH MULTIMEDIA!

BUT HUMANS ALSO MADE AN ASTOUNDING INVENTION: A WAY TO CREATE LASTING IMAGES! AND THE ORGAN WE USED WAS PRETTY UNLIKELY...

THE HAND, GET IT?

SOMETIME BACK IN THE STONE AGE, OUR ANCESTORS LEARNED TO MOLD CLAY INTO STATUES...

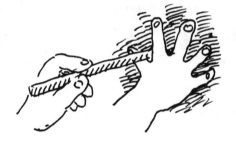

AND TRACE THE OUTLINES OF VARIOUS THINGS ONTO SURFACES — IN OTHER WORDS, TO DRAW AND SCULPT!

THE FIRST PIECE OF IMAGE PROCESSING TECHNOLOGY WAS — THE CRAYON!

I MAY NOT KNOW MUCH ABOUT ART, BUT I KNOW WHAT I LIKE TO EAT!

ONCE PEOPLE STARTED DRAWING, THE HISTORY OF VISUALS SPLIT ALONG THESE LINES:

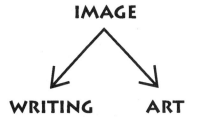

ON THE WRITING SIDE, STORY-TELLERS BEGAN USING PICTOGRAPHS: **ICONS** REPRESENTING THINGS AND EVENTS...

WHICH EVOLVED INTO WRITING SYSTEMS LIKE HIEROGLYPHICS, WHICH LOOK LIKE PICTURES, BUT WERE REALLY SYMBOLS FOR SOUNDS.

THE ALPHABET REDUCED THE NUMBER OF SYMBOLS TO FEWER THAN 30.

FINALLY, THE LAST VESTIGES OF REPRESENTATION WERE SQUEEZED OUT, AND THE ALPHABET BECAME A SET OF COMPLETELY CONVENTIONAL SYMBOLS.

MEANWHILE, OVER ON THE ART SIDE, PAINTERS PUTTERED AROUND WITH MATERIALS AND TECHNIQUES!

IT WASN'T LONG BEFORE THE MULTIMEDIA TYPES GOT INTO THE ACT, TRYING TO CLOSE THE DIAGRAM:

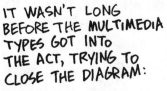

WRITING   ART

EARLY MULTIMEDIA

AS FAR AS I KNOW, THE FIRST MULTIMEDIA ARTISTS IN THE WEST WERE MONKS MAKING ILLUMINATED MANUSCRIPTS, IN WHICH THE RICH ILLUSTRATIONS IMPART A SACRED GLOW TO THE WHOLE.

EVENTUALLY, THE SCRIPT STYLE ITSELF ACQUIRED THIS MEANING...

IN CHINA, WHERE WRITING IS ESSENTIALLY PICTORIAL, WORDS AND PICTURES ARE WRITTEN WITH THE SAME BRUSH. THERE THEY HAVE A UNITY UNKNOWN IN THE WEST. CHINESE CALLIGRAPHY IS A HIGH ART, AND CHINESE MUSEUM-GOERS DO SOMETHING YOU RARELY SEE AMONG EUROPEANS: THEY IMITATE THE ARTIST'S GESTURES— A **KINESTHETIC** RESPONSE TO ART!!

THEN CAME

printing
printing
Printing

THE FAMOUS NAME IS
GUTENBERG,
INVENTOR OF MOVABLE
TYPE, OIL-BASED INK, AND
OTHER TECHNOLOGICAL
ADVANCES. AS NO PORTRAIT
OF GUTENBERG EXISTS,
HERE IS A PICTURE OF A
PRESS INSTEAD.

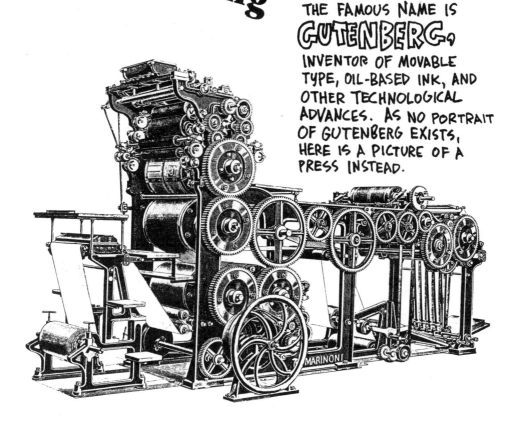

PRINTING MADE LANGUAGE INTO
SOMETHING PERFECTLY
REPRODUCIBLE...IT DEMOCRATIZED
LITERATURE... NOW EVERYONE COULD
HAVE TEXTBOOKS...EVERYONE COULD
READ THE BIBLE, IF NOT IN
GUTENBERG'S MASSIVE EDITION,
THEN IN THE CHEAP, ILLUSTRATED
VERSIONS CALLED "PAUPER'S
BIBLES." (THESE ARE NOW ALMOST
AS RARE AS GUTENBERG'S PORTRAIT.)

THE FIRST
COMIC BOOKS!

IN THE 1700'S AND 1800'S CAME THE ILLUSTRATED MAGAZINES... THE JOURNALS OF CARICATURE... THE ENGRAVINGS AND LITHOGRAPHS OF HOGARTH, DAUMIER, NAST...

THEN — THE REVOLUTION!!

SMILE, LOOK CASUAL, AND DON'T MOVE FOR SIXTY SECONDS...

PHOTOGRAPHY: HERE AT LAST, IT SEEMED, WAS A TECHNOLOGY FOR CAPTURING REALITY. PAINTERS SCRAMBLED TO FIND NEW REASONS TO PAINT, OR ELSE FACE OBSOLESCENCE... THEY INVENTED IMPRESSIONISM, EXPRESSIONISM, FAUVISM, CUBISM, AND OTHER ISMS... NOW PAINTING HAD TO BE "ABOUT PAINT" AS WELL AS ABOUT REALITY.

ON THE OTHER HAND, THE PHOTOGRAPH'S "REALITY" WAS OF AN UNFAMILIAR KIND... ITS BORDERS COULD BE CROPPED IN ANY NUMBER OF WAYS... IT EXISTS IN NO DISCERNIBLE CONTEXT... IT CREATES ITS OWN CONTEXT... IT LOOKS LIKE REALITY, BUT IT EXISTS OUTSIDE REALITY, IN THE SENSE THAT REALITY IS AN INTERDEPENDENT MATRIX OF EVENTS, WITH A HISTORY, CAUSES AND EFFECTS — IN A WORD, CONNECTEDNESS.

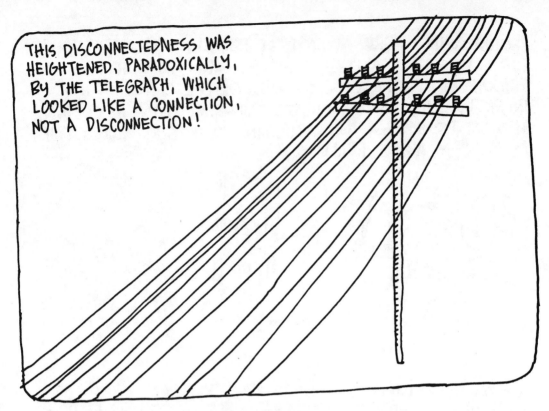

THIS DISCONNECTEDNESS WAS HEIGHTENED, PARADOXICALLY, BY THE TELEGRAPH, WHICH LOOKED LIKE A CONNECTION, NOT A DISCONNECTION!

WHAT WAS DISCONNECTED WAS THE SEQUENCE OF EVENTS THAT THE TELEGRAPH DELIVERED...

MOTHERS GRIEVE FAR AWAY!

EXPLORER GOES SOMEPLACE UNIMPORTANT!

ITALIAN GOVERNMENT FALLS!

UTRECHT RESIDENT INJURED IN NUCLEAR HOLOCAUST!

THE CONCEPT OF NEWS WAS BORN.

...WHICH BRINGS US TO TELEVISION...

TELEVISION IS THE ULTIMATE DISCONNECTOR. AS NEIL POSTMAN POINTS OUT IN HIS POLEMICAL BOOK, "AMUSING OURSELVES TO DEATH," TELEVISION HAS INTRODUCED A NEW ENGLISH PHRASE WHICH EXPRESSES A COMPLETE **ABSENCE OF ANY CONNECTION** BETWEEN ONE THING AND THE NEXT: "NOW THIS."

AX-MURDER SUSPECT LEADS POLICE TO GRISLY MASS GRAVE. FILM AT ELEVEN. NOW THIS...

119

DON'T GET ME WRONG... T.V. IS GREAT! IT TAKES US TO PLACES WE'D NEVER GO WITHOUT IT...

WHAT **ARE** THEY THINKING??

AS A WELL-MEANING PARENT, I OFTEN TURN OFF THE SOUND DURING COMMERCIALS. SO I KNOW AT FIRST HAND WHAT MORE SOPHISTICATED OBSERVERS HAVE DISCOVERED: THE SOUND BARELY MATTERS! SOMEHOW THOSE KIDS GET

EVERYTHING!!

THE DOLL WITH BLUE SKIN IS LADY LOVELILOCKS' EVIL ENEMY BLACKTHORNE AND SHE HAS A PURPLE PONY NAMED SUPERNOVA...

IMAGES OVERWHELM WORDS.

NO ONE UNDERSTOOD THIS BETTER THAN FORMER PRESIDENT **REAGAN'S** "MEDIA HANDLERS."

WHEN THE GOVERNMENT CUT ITS SUPPORT FOR NURSING HOMES, FOR EXAMPLE, PRES. REAGAN WAS FILMED VISITING A NURSING HOME. THE FILM APPEARED ON T.V., AND, LO, THE BAD NEWS FADED...

BUT THE TRULY FRIGHTENING PART IS: A REPORTER MADE A DOCUMENTARY EXPOSING THE PRACTICE. OF COURSE, THE DOCUMENTARY SHOWED THE "MANIPULATIVE" FILM OF REAGAN'S NURSING-HOME VISIT — AND SO PEOPLE **STILL** STILL BELIEVED THAT REAGAN SUPPORTED NURSING HOMES — OVER 50% OF THE VIEWERS, ACCORDING TO THE T.V. NETWORK'S OWN SURVEY!!

ANOTHER EXAMPLE, CLOSER TO HOME (FOR ME), WAS

THE QUAKE OF '89.

IN OCTOBER, 1989,
NORTHERN CALIFORNIA
WAS ROCKED BY AN
EARTHQUAKE. I WAS
THERE, AND I COULDN'T
HELP COMPARING THE
SITUATION "ON THE GROUND"
WITH WHAT WE WERE
SEEING "ON THE AIR."

BUT THE T.V. NETWORKS BROADCAST THE SAME THREE IMAGES
OVER AND OVER AND OVER: A COLLAPSED FREEWAY, A RUINED
NEIGHBORHOOD, AND A DAMAGED BRIDGE.

NOT THAT THERE WASN'T MAJOR DAMAGE — THERE WAS — BUT WHERE WAS THE ANALYSIS, THE ATTEMPT TO PUT THIS EARTHQUAKE IN PERSPECTIVE, TO COMPARE IT WITH OTHER, SIMILAR QUAKES? WHERE WERE THE IMAGES OF MORE TYPICAL NEIGHBORHOODS? AND WHERE WAS ANYTHING ABOUT SANTA CRUZ AND WATSONVILLE, TWO TOWNS 100 MILES TO THE SOUTH, WHICH HAD REALLY BEEN DEVASTATED?

AND, WHEN THE SAME THREE IMAGES KEPT REPEATING, WHY DIDN'T ANYONE CONCLUDE THAT THE REASON MIGHT BE BECAUSE THERE WAS NO OTHER LARGE-SCALE DAMAGE IN SAN FRANCISCO??

WHY DOES THIS HAPPEN? WHY DO IMAGES HIT US SO HARD?

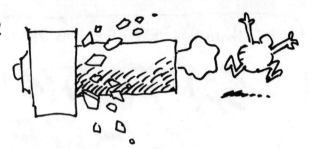

I THINK IT HAS SOMETHING TO DO WITH THE FACT THAT IMAGE-PROJECTION, UNLIKE LANGUAGE, IS AN UNNATURAL ACT...

WHEN WE PROCESS LANGUAGE, OUR BRAINS KNOW IT'S ONLY WORDS. WE MAY EVEN STOP AND THINK ABOUT IT!

BUT IMAGE-PROJECTION IS NOT BIOLOGICAL! WHEN WE SEE AN IMAGE, WE DO NOT INSTINCTIVELY REACT AS IF IT'S ARTIFICIAL. AT THE REPTILE LEVEL, WE TAKE IMAGES AS IF THEY WERE **REALITY!**

CHAPTER 8
SEEING IS BELIEVING?

A BEAM OF LIGHT BOUNCES OFF AN OBJECT "OUT THERE..." IT BENDS THROUGH YOUR SPECS, STRUGGLES INTO THE LIQUID INTERIOR OF AN EYEBALL DISTORTED BY AGE AND BAD READING HABITS, AND FALLS, FINALLY, UPSIDE-DOWN ON THE FRAYED RECEPTIVE SURFACE OF YOUR RETINA... PHEW!

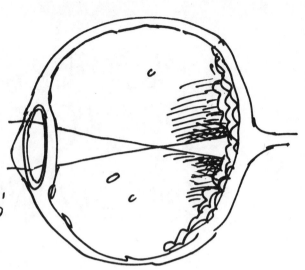

FROM THERE AN ELECTRIC SIGNAL PASSES UP THE OPTIC NERVES TO YOUR BRAIN, WHICH, IN SOME MYSTERIOUS WAY, PROCESSES THE INFORMATION INTO... SOMETHING... THAT WE CALL A **MENTAL IMAGE**...

IMAGE, THAT IS, AS OPPOSED TO REALITY... AND WE SAY, "SEEING IS BELIEVING"??

RIGHT. I DON'T BELIEVE IN REALITY.

126

FOR EXAMPLE, WE ARE EVOLUTIONARILY PROGRAMMED TO SEE THINGS. IT'S OBVIOUS WHY: WE EAT THINGS...

AND THINGS EAT US!

BECAUSE OF THIS, WE LIKE TO SEE OUTLINES.

IN FACT, WE LIKE OUTLINES SO MUCH THAT OUR MIND FILLS THEM IN WHEN THEY AREN'T EVEN THERE!!

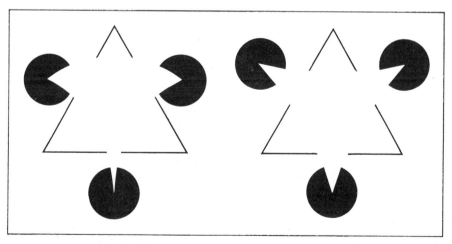

I HOPE THAT YOU SEE THE CURVED, WHITE, TRIANGULAR "THINGS." I KNOW I DO!!

IS IT EDIBLE?

IMAGE, IMAGINE, IMAGINATION, IMAGINARY... THESE WORDS REMIND US HOW FAR REALITY IS FROM VISUAL INFORMATION.

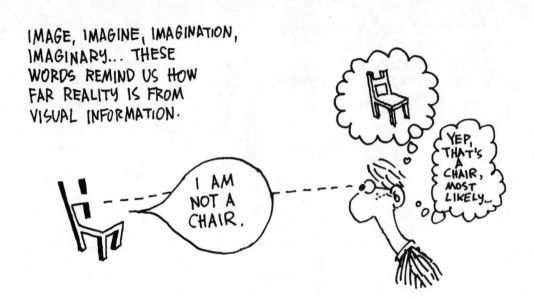

THE ACT OF SEEING IS JUST THAT—AN **ACT**, WITH THE BRAIN DOING MOST OF THE ACTING. MORE THAN WE REALIZE, WE SEE WITH OUR MIND'S EYE.

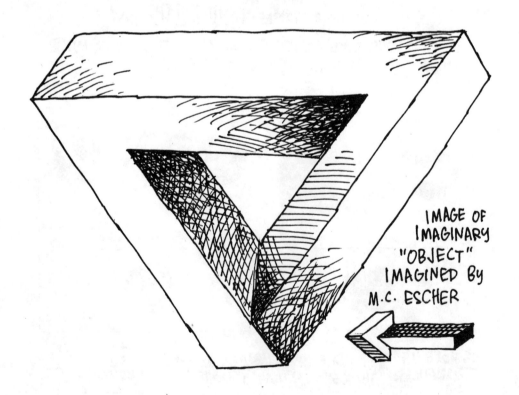

IMAGE OF IMAGINARY "OBJECT" IMAGINED BY M.C. ESCHER

WHITER THAN WHITE!

(BY THE WAY, YOU MAY ALSO NOTICE THAT THE IMAGINARY WHITE FIGURES ALSO APPEAR BRIGHTER THAN THE SURROUNDING WHITE BACKGROUND!)

→ SUBJECTIVE OUTLINES, OPTICAL ILLUSIONS, FACES SEEN IN PATTERNS OF LINE OR SHADOW, FALSE PERSPECTIVE, "JUMPING" QUILT PATTERNS — ALL THESE ARE EVIDENCE OF THE MIND'S ACTIVE ROLE IN VISION.

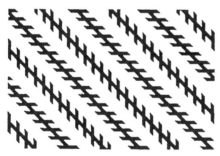

PARALLEL DIAGONALS

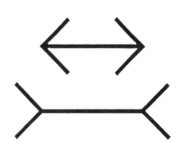

EQUAL HORIZONTALS

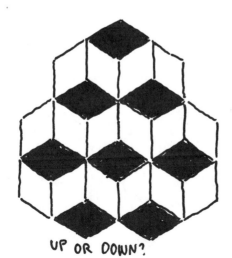

UP OR DOWN?

I'M KIND OF AN ILLUSION MYSELF!

THIS IS ONE SIDE OF THE "SEEING IS BELIEVING" PROBLEM. WE SEE WHAT WE WANT, OR AT LEAST WHAT WE EXPECT.

A GIANT!

THE OTHER SIDE IS THE THRIVING BUSINESS THAT EXISTS IN IMAGE MANAGEMENT. WHAT YOU SEE, SOMEONE ELSE MADE!

LOOK AT THESE STUNNING BUDGET FIGURES! WHOLLY IMAGINARY!!

BUT...SO... VISIBLE...

1997 1999

SO WE HAVE THE FAMILIAR ONSLAUGHT OF IMAGES, ARRIVING TOO FAST TO ASSIMILATE, EXPLOITING OUR BRAINS' ABILITY TO FILL IN THE DETAILS.

SOUNDS PRETTY HOPELESS, DOESN'T IT? WITH ALL THAT DISTORTION, MANIPULATION, AND SELECTIVE PERCEPTION GOING ON, WHAT'S THE FUTURE — AND THE POINT — OF VISUAL COMMUNICATION?

YES, VISUAL COMMUNICATION IS HOT — AND LET'S FACE IT: 50,000 BUDDING PRODUCERS CAN'T BE WRONG!! IMAGERY **CAN** BE AN EFFECTIVE WAY TO CONVEY INFORMATION!

FOR EXAMPLE:

ENTERTAINMENT

FACE IT: SOMETIMES EMOTIONAL IMAGERY IS JUST WHAT WE WANT TO SEE. CALL IT ART!

: SOB! : THOSE "LEAVE IT TO BEAVER" RERUNS JUST TEAR ME APART!

O N THE OTHER HAND, THIS IMAGERY ASSAULTS US CONTINUALLY, WHETHER WE LIKE IT OR NOT... PLUS IT'S ADDICTIVE. T.V. INVITES US TO FLIP THROUGH A ZILLION CHANNELS, EACH ONE JERKING OUR RESPONSES IN A ZILLION DIFFERENT DIRECTIONS, DRAWING US INTO A WORLD THAT WOULD DRIVE ANY SELF-RESPECTING REPTILE CRAZY.

JIBBER
JIBBER
JIBBER

CLIK
CLIK
CLIK

TRAINING AND EDUCATION

IMAGES ARE "MORE REAL" THAN WORDS, SO IMAGES CAN TEACH VERY EFFECTIVELY. I COULD GO ON AND ON ABOUT THIS (IT'S MY JOB, AFTER ALL), BUT FOR THE TIME BEING, I'LL ONLY ASK: IF YOU WERE LEARNING HOW TO OPERATE A NUCLEAR REACTOR, WOULD YOU RATHER BE READING A TEXT-ONLY MANUAL, OR SITTING IN A MULTIMEDIA SIMULATOR??

NEXT TIME, USE THE SIMULATOR!

ON THE OTHER HAND, IT'S EASY TO OVERUSE OR MISUSE IMAGES. DIAGRAMS CAN BE CONFUSING, IMAGE AND TEXT MAY NOT MATCH, AND CARTOON CHARACTERS ARE OFTEN TACKED ON TO "MAKE LEARNING FUN" WITHOUT REGARD FOR CONTENT, BECOMING AN ANNOYING DISTRACTION INSTEAD OF AN AID TO LEARNING.

LIKE ME! I'M ABSOLUTELY USELESS!

REPRESENTING DATA

WE EXCEL AT PERCEIVING PATTERNS.*
THIS MEANS THAT A MASS OF STATISTICAL
DATA HAS MORE MEANING AND
IMPACT WHEN PRESENTED GRAPHICALLY.

SPACE DEBRIS

object	altitude	latitude	longitude
bolt	373 km	37°56'08" N	187°09'33"
wrench	186 km	9°17'14" N	14°34'01"
cable	1563 km	18°44'43" S	27°22'49"
helmet	999 km	65°03'55" N	89°17'15"
reactor	2754 km	44°58'22" S	279°38'49"
bolt	3344 km	43°29'08" N	65°43'22"
pliers	784 km	34°06'41" N	189°41'23"
paper			

BUT OF COURSE, GRAPHICS CAN EQUALLY WELL **MIS**REPRESENT
DATA. FOR COMPLETE DETAILS, SEE TWO WONDERFUL BOOKS
BY EDWARD TUFTE: THE VISUAL DISPLAY OF QUANTITATIVE
INFORMATION AND ENVISIONING INFORMATION. A TYPICAL
EXAMPLE IS A GRAPH WITH ONE AXIS DISTORTED TO MAKE
A MORE DRAMATIC IMPRESSION:

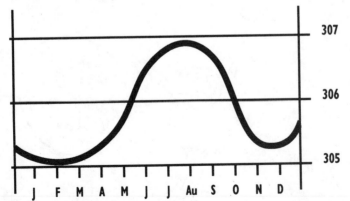

N.B. X-AXIS
IS NOT AT
ZERO, SO SMALL
CHANGES IN THE
CURVE LOOK
BIG.

*IN FACT, WE'RE A LITTLE TOO GOOD AT IT; SOMETIMES WE SEE PATTERNS
WHERE THERE AREN'T ANY!

SIMULATION

THANKS TO THE COMPUTER, CHEMISTS CAN VISUALIZE MOLECULES IN 3 DIMENSIONS; ARCHITECTS CAN TRANSFORM BLUEPRINTS INTO DYNAMIC IMAGES OF BUILDINGS; GRAPHIC DESIGNERS CAN WHIP UP FULL-COLOR MOCK-UPS OF PAGES IN NO TIME. IT'S UNQUESTIONABLY GREAT: A FABULOUS TOOL FOR EMPOWERING OUR IMAGINATIONS!

THE DOWNSIDE HERE IS THAT IT'S **SO** EASY TO MAKE CHANGES THAT EVERYONE CAN GET INTO THE ACT, AND THE DESIGNER'S ORIGINAL VISION (IF ANY) CAN EASILY SUCCUMB TO DESIGN BY COMMITTEE.

VIDEOCONFERENCING

SIMULATES A FACE-TO-FACE MEETING
BY ALLOWING A TELEPHONE CONFERENCE
CALL THAT INCLUDES LIVE VIDEO IMAGES
OF EVERYONE ON EVERYONE ELSE'S SCREEN.
IT'S A PHONE CALL WITH BODY LANGUAGE!

BUT CONSIDER THE ADVANTAGES OF ELECTRONIC MAIL **WITHOUT**
VISUALS: IN THE ABSENCE OF A FACE, PEOPLE RESPOND TO
EACH OTHER BASED PURELY ON THE CONTENT (AND STYLE)
OF THEIR MESSAGES, REGARDLESS OF PREJUDICIAL ISSUES
LIKE RACE, APPEARANCE, AGE, GENDER, ETC.

SO — IS SEEING BELIEVING?
BY NOW, THE ANSWER SHOULD
BE CLEAR: SOMETIMES IT IS,
AND SOMETIMES IT ISN'T!

· CHAPTER 9 ·

IN THE LAST CHAPTER, WE SAW SOME COMPELLING REASONS FOR PURSUING VISUAL COMMUNICATION. BESIDES THOSE, THERE IS ANOTHER REASON SO MANY PEOPLE ARE CHASING THE GRAIL OF MULTIMEDIA: BECAUSE TECHNOLOGY LETS THEM DO IT! ANYONE ARMED WITH A VIDEO CAMERA AND A COMPUTER CAN BE AN IMAGE-MANIPULATION MOGUL. SOON, THE PRODUCERS WILL OUTNUMBER THE CONSUMERS!

THE CONCLUSION IS HARD TO ESCAPE: IN THE FUTURE, WE'LL BE SPENDING MORE TIME IN FRONT OF THE GLOWING BOX!

IN LIGHT OF ALL WE KNOW ABOUT TV'S EFFECTS — PASSIVITY, ISOLATION, DISCONNECTION OF REALITY, ETC. ETC. — IT'S WORTH ASKING WHETHER THE COMPUTER IS COMING TO THE RESCUE, OR IS IT JUST GOING TO MAKE EVERYTHING WORSE??

THE OBVIOUS SIMILARITIES BETWEEN THE COMPUTER AND THE T.V. ARE PRETTY SUPERFICIAL: THEY'RE BOTH BOXY AND USE A DISPLAY SCREEN. BUT BEYOND THOSE ARE SOME EQUALLY OBVIOUS DIFFERENCES:

TO BEGIN WITH, AT THE MOST BASIC LEVEL, A COMPUTER DEMANDS LOGICAL THOUGHT FROM THE USER, WHILE THE T.V. DEMANDS NOTHING AT ALL... THE COMPUTER USER HAS AN ACTIVE STANCE TOWARD THE MACHINE, UNLIKE THE TELEVISION "USER." THIS CAN COME AS A SHOCK TO SOMEONE WEANED ON T.V...

THAT'S WHAT THE COMPUTER IS. IT FORCES THE USER OUT OF HIS T.V.-INDUCED TRANCE AND INTO AN ACTIVE ENGAGEMENT WITH THE MACHINE.

EVEN "MINDLESS" VIDEO GAMES DEVELOP QUICK REFLEXES!

AT A SLIGHTLY HIGHER LEVEL, COMPUTER GRAPHICS ARE VERY USEFUL FOR MAKING SENSE OF IMPORTANT BUSINESS INFORMATION.

AT THE MOST SOPHISTICATED LEVEL, COMPUTER GRAPHICS
HAVE CREATED AN ENTIRELY NEW KIND OF SCIENTIFIC AND
MATHEMATICAL EXPLORATION: THE VISUAL SIMULATION OF
COMPLEX PROCESSES. THE COMPUTER CAN SIMULATE THE
WEATHER, A PROTEIN, A NUCLEAR EXPLOSION, AN ECONOMY.
MATHEMATICIANS LIKE TO PLAY WITH THE INFINITELY WIGGLY
OBJECT CALLED THE MANDELBRODT SET:

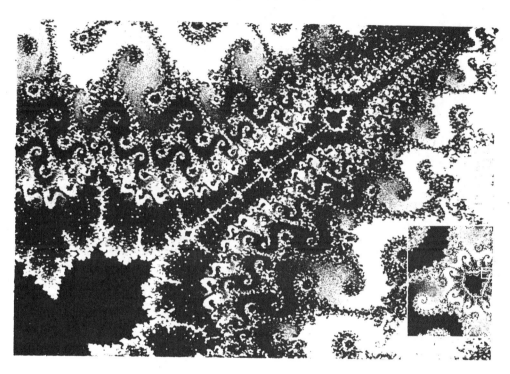

COMPUTERS CAN
ALSO SIMULATE
ARTIFICIAL
"WORLDS" WITH
HYPOTHETICAL LAWS.
IF YOU CAN
INVENT IT,
NOW YOU CAN
SEE IT!

IT'S WEDDING SOFTWARE FOR A PLANET WITH FOURTEEN SEXES.

NOW COMES THE STRANGE PART!

THE SIMILARITIES BETWEEN THE TV AND THE COMPUTER ARE SUPERFICIAL... BUT, STRIKING AS THEY MAY SEEM, SO ARE THE DIFFERENCES! AT THE FUNDAMENTAL LEVEL, THE TWO APPLIANCES ARE ABOUT TO MERGE INTO A SINGLE HYBRID OBJECT!

IT'S AN IDENTITY CRISIS!

TV PROGRAMS? NOTHING BUT INFORMATION!

AND ALL INFORMATION CAN BE DIGITALLY ENCODED, I.E., PUT IN COMPUTER-USABLE FORM. IT SO HAPPENS THAT TV SIGNALS ARE NOT YET DIGITAL, BUT IT'S ONLY A MATTER OF TIME, AND WHEN THAT HAPPENS, YOUR T.V. CAN BECOME A COMPUTER!!

146

ALREADY, PROFESSIONAL VIDEO PRODUCTION INCORPORATES PLENTY OF DIGITAL TECHNOLOGY. IMAGES ARE DIGITALLY CREATED, EDITED, AND MANIPULATED.

OUCH!

IN THE NEAR FUTURE, THE T.V. RECEIVER WILL ALSO HAVE A COMPUTER INSTALLED, MAKING IT A **SMART T.V.!!**

SMART T.V.? NOW THERE'S A CONTRADICTION IN TERMS...

THIS WILL MAKE IT POSSIBLE FOR THE VIEWER—OR USER—TO INTERACT WITH THE SET.

I **SAID**—WHAT WOULD YOU LIKE TO WATCH TODAY?

NOBODY KNOWS EXACTLY WHAT INTERACTIVE T.V. WILL LOOK LIKE, BUT HERE IT COMES!!

THE SCENARIO GOES LIKE THIS: THE "SMART T.V." WILL BE CONNECTED TO A WORLDWIDE NETWORK OF DIGITAL INFORMATION. EVERYTHING — AND EVERYONE — WILL BE ON LINE.

YOU WANT INFORMATION? THE SMART T.V. WILL GET IT!

YOU WANT TO WATCH A MOVIE? THE SMART T.V. WILL DOWNLOAD IT!

YOU WANT TO PLAY A VIDEO GAME?

VISIT WITH A FRIEND?

READ A BOOK? LISTEN TO A SYMPHONY? GO TO A FOOTBALL GAME?

YOU WANT SOME EXERCISE?

SO WHAT'S GOING TO HAPPEN TO COMMUNICATION WHEN THE T.V. GETS INTELLIGENT? WILL ALL OF US PASSIVE VIDEO CONSUMERS MAGICALLY BECOME ACTIVE VIDEO COMMUNICATORS?

YAWN... IT'S TIME TO GET MORE INVOLVED... THINK I'LL CHANGE THE CHANNEL...

IT'S CERTAINLY POSSIBLE... BUT IT ISN'T NECESSARY! AFTER ALL, ONE ASPECT OF THE SMART TV'S INTELLIGENCE IS TO UNDERSTAND YOUR TASTES AND ANTICIPATE YOUR NEEDS. IN COMPUTER JARGON, YOUR TELEVISION/COMPUTER WILL BECOME YOUR "INTELLIGENT AGENT," BRINGING YOU THE RIGHT INFORMATION (DATA, STORIES, SHOWS, REMINDERS, ETC) WITHOUT BEING ASKED !!

HEY! DON'T DO **THAT!** I HAVE **JUST** WHAT YOU **WANT!**

BUT—

YES, ONE FUTURE ROLE OF THE COMPUTER IS TO KNOW *EVERYTHING* ON TELEVISION !!

MY T.V. SET IS MORE INTELLIGENT THAN I AM...

THIS MEANS, OF COURSE, THAT WE'LL HAVE TO LEARN HOW TO COMMUNICATE WITH OUR TELEVISIONS...

AND I NEVER LEARNED TO PROGRAM MY VCR!

IT'S NOT ONLY TELEVISIONS... COMPUTERS ARE ALSO MERGING WITH OTHER APPLIANCES, BRINGING INTERACTIVITY TO A NEW LEVEL!

PSST! ARTHUR!

WHEN THAT HAPPENS, WHAT'S TO STOP THE SMART APPLIANCES FROM TALKING TO EACH OTHER?

ARTHUR, THIS IS TOM, YOUR TOASTER! WHY HAVEN'T I HEARD FROM YOU LATELY?

AS ARTHUR'S STOVE, I KNOW IT'S BECAUSE ARTHUR IS BASICALLY SELFISH AND UNCARING...

DON'T TALK ABOUT ARTHUR THIS WAY, WHEN HE'S IN THE ROOM...

IT LOOKS AS IF BEFORE WE CAN COMMUNICATE WITH EACH OTHER, WE'LL HAVE TO COMMUNICATE WITH THE COMMUNICATION EQUIPMENT!

REMEMBER, INTELLIGENT TELEVISION IS SOMETHING DIFFERENT FROM INTELLIGENT PROGRAMMING.
MORE "BRADY BUNCH" RERUNS!

· CHAPTER 10 ·
RESOLUTION NOW!

Just as the computer compels us to think about information rather than meaning, it also drives people (mostly male people, admittedly) to look for technical solutions to communications problems.

I'M NOT GETTING THROUGH TO YOU, DOROTHY! WHERE'S MY SCREWDRIVER?

IN ITS RAWEST FORM, THIS QUEST BECOMES A SIMPLE PURSUIT OF FASTER, MORE POWERFUL COMPUTERS.

MORE RAM! MORE MIPS! MORE MEGAFLOPS!

WELL, IT ISN'T SURPRISING; GRAPHICS REQUIRE LOTS OF COMPUTER POWER, AND THE HIGHER THE **RESOLUTION,** THE MORE POWER YOU NEED!

RESOLUTION? WOTS DOT?

YA! DOT'S DOTS! DOTS LOTSA DOTS!

THE WORD RESOLUTION REFERS TO THE LEVEL OF DETAIL A PIECE OF EQUIPMENT CAN HANDLE. IT'S USED IN THE SAME SENSE AS THE RESOLUTION OF A LENS. THE HIGHER THE RESOLUTION, THE FINER THE DETAILS YOU CAN SEE.

AT THE LOW END OF THE RESOLUTION SCALE, A COMPUTER MONITOR MAY HAVE 72 "PIXELS," OR PICTURE ELEMENTS, PER INCH, EACH PIXEL EITHER ALL WHITE OR ALL BLACK. FINE DETAILS ARE LOST...

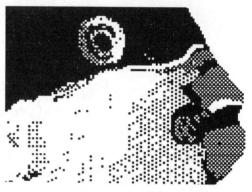

AT THE HIGH END, A COLOR IMAGESETTER PRODUCES OUTPUT OF MORE THAN 2500 DOTS PER INCH, WITH OVER 16 MILLION COLORS AVAILABLE FOR EACH DOT— TOTAL PHOTO REALISM !!

WOW! TOO BAD YOU CAN'T SEE THIS!

NOW LET'S DO A LITTLE ARITHMETIC. IN EACH SQUARE INCH, THE HIGH-RESOLUTION PRINTER MAKES ROUGHLY

$$2500 \times 2500 = 6.25 \text{ MILLION DOTS.}$$

EACH DOT GETS TO CHOOSE FROM (TO BE PRECISE) 16,777,216 COLORS, SO THE TOTAL NUMBER OF POSSIBLE ARRANGEMENTS OF COLORED DOTS IS

$$(16,777,216)^{6,250,000}$$

HELP! A GIGANTIC NUMBER!

WHEW!

THIS IS THE TOTAL NUMBER OF ONE-SQUARE-INCH-SIZED IMAGES WHICH CAN BE DISPLAYED AT THAT RESOLUTION.

* * * * * * * * * * *

HOW BIG IS DOT?

WELL, IT'S ABOUT $2^{150,000,000}$ ... SO IN COMPUTER-SPEAK WE SAY THERE ARE **150 MILLION BITS** OF INFORMATION IN THAT LITTLE IMAGE.

WHETHER YOU FOLLOWED THE MATH OR NOT, YOU'LL PROBABLY AGREE THAT 150 MILLION BITS IS A LOAD OF INFORMATION* — AND THAT WAS JUST FOR ONE SQUARE INCH!

*ABOUT 20 MEGABYTES

NOW IMAGINE ANIMATING THE IMAGE... YOU'D HAVE TO PILE UP AT LEAST A **DOZEN** OF THESE PICTURES EVERY SECOND...

150 MILLION BITS
150 MILLION BITS
150 MILLION BITS
150 MILLION BITS
150 MILLION BITS
150 MILLION BITS
150 MILLION BITS
150 MILLION BITS
150 MILLION BITS

THIS GIVES ME A NEW APPRECIATION OF MICKEY MOUSE!

AND IF YOU WANTED TO MAKE A FULLY COMPUTER-GENERATED 3-DIMENSIONAL ENVIRONMENT—?!

OBVIOUSLY, HIGH-RESOLUTION IMAGE-PROCESSING TAKES PLENTY OF COMPUTER POWER... AND NOW THAT WE HAVE A NUMERICAL ESTIMATE OF HOW MUCH, WE MIGHT ASK: IS A PICTURE REALLY WORTH A THOUSAND WORDS?

IN STANDARD COMPUTER CODE, EACH LETTER OF THE ALPHABET IS SPECIFIED BY **EIGHT** BITS, SO THIS 5-LETTER WORD NEEDS $5 \times 8 = 40$ BITS.

COMPARING WORD AND IMAGE — IMAGE WITH 150 MILLION BITS, WORD WITH 40, WE DIVIDE TO FIND

$$150,000,000 \div 40 = 3,750,000$$

IN OTHER WORDS, FROM THE COMPUTER'S POINT OF VIEW, ONE HIGH-RESOLUTION PICTURE IS WORTH ALMOST

4 MILLION WORDS!

THERE'S SOMETHING FISHY ABOUT THIS CALCULATION. COULD A PICTURE REALLY BE WORTH FOUR MILLION WORDS??

FOUR MILLION BONES, MAYBE!

IF YOU DOUBLE THE RESOLUTION, IS A PICTURE SUDDENLY WORTH **EIGHT** MILLION WORDS? IF YOU UPPED THE RESOLUTION BY A FACTOR OF A THOUSAND (IT'S TECHNICALLY POSSIBLE!) WOULD THE PICTURE BECOME THE EQUIVALENT OF

8 BILLION

WORDS?? IT'S ABSURD, ESPECIALLY CONSIDERING THAT YOU WOULDN'T BE ABLE TO SEE ANY DIFFERENCE !!!

WORDS FAIL ME.

ONE SQUARE INCH

THIS SILLY ARITHMETIC SHOWS HOW MISGUIDED THE TECHNICAL QUEST CAN BE. OBVIOUSLY, YOU CAN PILE ON TONS MORE INFORMATION WITHOUT ADDING ANOTHER OUNCE OF MEANING!!

ACHIEVING DEEP MEANING WITH A SCREW-DRIVER, THAT'S MY CHALLENGE!

TO BE SURE, ULTRAHIGH RESOLUTION GRAPHICS HAS ITS PLACE IN FILM, IN EXTREME MINIATURIZATION, AND ELSEWHERE, BUT IN MOST ORDINARY COMMUNICATION, IT'S OVERKILL!

AND THESE BIG MONITORS WEIGH A TON!

SO LET'S LEAVE THE TECHNOWIZARDS TO RESOLVE THE RESOLUTION PROBLEM (AND THEN FIGURE OUT HOW TO RESOLVE THEIR OWN DIFFERENCES)...

WHY DOES CARTOONING WORK? BECAUSE YOU, DEAR READER, FILL IN MOST OF THE DETAILS! REMEMBER, SEEING IS AN ACTIVE PROCESS; THE BRAIN IS AT WORK AS WELL AS THE EYES... AND THE CARTOONIST EXPLOITS THIS FACT BY DRAWING NO MORE THAN NECESSARY TO CONVEY THE ESSENTIAL IDEA. YOU DO THE REST!!

THE IDEA IS NOT TO "SIMPLIFY" THE IMAGE — THAT SUGGESTS OMITTING SOMETHING IMPORTANT — BUT TO STRIP THE IMAGE DOWN TO ITS BARE ESSENTIALS.

TO ILLUSTRATE THE POWER OF CARTOONS, RESEARCH DONE AT M.I.T. SHOWED THAT WE RECOGNIZE CELEBRITY FACES FASTER FROM A CARICATURE THAN FROM A PHOTOGRAPH!! IT REALLY IS POSSIBLE TO DO MORE WITH LESS...

BECAUSE YOU, DEAR READER, SUPPLY SO MUCH, YOU'RE MORE "IN THE PICTURE" THAN WITH HIGH-RESOLUTION GRAPHICS, WHICH DEMAND LITTLE OF YOUR BRAIN...

WHOA!

PARENTHETICALLY

(THE MENTAL PROCESSING IS AN EFFORT, WHICH EXPLAINS WHY READING A "SIMPLE" COMIC BOOK CAN SEEM LIKE A LOT OF WORK, IF YOU AREN'T IN SHAPE.)

UNH! PAGE 2!

BECAUSE YOUR BRAIN IS MAKING MOST OF IT UP, YOU TEND TO IDENTIFY MORE WITH CARTOONS THAN WITH OTHER IMAGES. THIS MAKES THE CARTOON A USER-FRIENDLY MEDIUM.

EXCEPT FOR ME— I HATE MYSELF!

IN FACT, I HAVE A HUNCH—AN UNSUBSTANTIATED HUNCH—THAT THE SMILE PEOPLE OFTEN DISPLAY WHEN LOOKING AT CARTOON CHARACTERS IS AKIN TO A BABY'S SMILE WHEN IT SEES A FACE, ANY FACE. IT'S A PRIMITIVE SMILE OF RECOGNITION!

YAAA

AN EXAMPLE OF USING THIS IDENTIFICATION FOR INSTRUCTIONAL PURPOSES COMES FROM A BOOK I DID WITH MARK WHEELIS CALLED "THE CARTOON GUIDE TO GENETICS."

THERE WE WANTED TO EXPLAIN A COMPLICATED TYPE OF ORGANIC MOLECULE CALLED AN **ENZYME**.

RATHER THAN USING A MASS OF VERBIAGE, OR DRAWING SCIENTIFIC DIAGRAMS, WE DECIDED TO DRAW A CARICATURE OF THE WAY AN ENZYME ACTUALLY LOOKS (OR WOULD LOOK, IF YOU COULD SEE ANYTHING THAT SMALL).

THE RESULT WAS SOMETHING THAT LOOKED LIKE THIS...

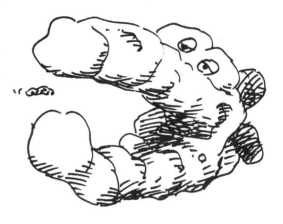

AND OCCASIONALLY DOES THIS:

NOTE THAT CARTOONING HAS ITS OWN LANGUAGE FOR EXPRESSING MOVEMENT!

THE RESULT IS (I BELIEVE) A MORE EFFECTIVE, INDELIBLE, AND (YES) REALISTIC EXPLANATION THAN ANYTHING FOUND IN CONVENTIONAL TEXTBOOKS OR HIGH-RESOLUTION COMPUTER-GENERATED MOLECULAR MODELS.

THE REASON—? IN THE CARTOON, THE ENZYME BECAME A **CHARACTER**.

A FRIENDLY, HUMANOID SORT OF BLOB!

A CARTOON CHARACTER IS LIKE A VERY SPECIAL FORM OF **ICON**: A **NARRATIVE** ICON, ONTO WHICH YOU PROJECT A PERSONALITY, A VOICE, AND AS MUCH HUMANITY AS YOU LIKE, IN AN ENZYME.

O.K.... I GET THE PICTURE!

A CARTOON CHARACTER CAN ILLUSTRATE ACTION...

HUP!

...REACT TO TEXT...

WITH TOTAL BOREDOM!

TOTAL

...ADD HUMOR...

AND WE CAN CREATE NARRATIVE CONTINUITY—GETTING YOU FROM HERE...

TO—

HEE

AS A PROJECTION OF YOUR MIND, CARTOON CHARACTERS
ARE ENDOWED WITH YOUR DESIRES, FEARS, AND EXPECTATIONS.
THEIR PLEASURES ARE YOUR PLEASURES... THEIR PAIN IS
YOUR PAIN.... WHATEVER HAPPENS TO THEM COULD
HAPPEN TO YOU.

BUT, AS MERE CARTOONS, THEY KNOW NO LIMITS! THEY
CAN DEFY THE LAWS OF PHYSICS... OR ANY OTHER LAWS.
SUBVERSIVE LITTLE ☆@#&s !!

WHAT'S THE RESOLUTION OF THE RESOLUTION QUESTION? WHAT'S IT TO BE, HIGH OR LOW? THE ANSWER HAS TO BE: BOTH.

COMMUNICATIONS IS BOTH A SCIENCE AND AN ART... THE ART IS IN FINDING THE MOST EFFECTIVE, ECONOMICAL, ELEGANT, AND ESSENTIAL WAYS TO CONVEY THE MESSAGE.

I HOPE SOMEONE IS LISTENING!

THE SUCCESS OF LOW-RESOLUTION MEDIA PROVES YOU CAN OFTEN DO WITHOUT SOPHISTICATED "COMMUNICATIONS EQUIPMENT."

ON THE OTHER HAND, HIGH TECHNOLOGY HAS ITS ATTRACTIONS, TOO...

SOMETIMES I LIKE TO DAYDREAM ABOUT THE PERFECT COMPUTER SYSTEM FOR MULTI-LEVEL COMMUNICATION...

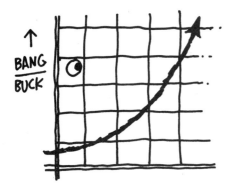

GOOD IMAGE-PROCESSING SOFTWARE IS ALREADY AVAILABLE FOR THE MICROCOMPUTER... THERE ARE PROGRAMS FOR GRAPHIC DESIGNERS AND ILLUSTRATORS...

THESE, COMBINED WITH THE LASER PRINTER, HAVE CREATED THE PHENOMENON OF DESKTOP PUBLISHING.

BUT THE ULTIMATE COMMUNICATION SYSTEM HAS YET TO ARRIVE... FOR EXAMPLE, SOME OF US STILL LOVE DIGGING AN INKY PEN POINT INTO A TOOTHY SHEET OF PAPER... THIS KINESTHETIC EXPERIENCE IS SOMETHING WE REFUSE TO GIVE UP!! FOR DIGITAL PROCESSING, WE NEED A FAST, VERY HIGH-RESOLUTION SCANNER

I CAN DREAM, CAN'T I?

TO DIGITIZE OUR DRAWINGS AND STORE THEM IN THE HUGE MEMORY OF OUR FULL-COLOR DESKTOP SUPERCOMPUTER!

AND HOW ABOUT SOME **TYPEFACE DESIGN** FEATURES, AND A HIGH-QUALITY **MUSIC** AND **SPEECH SYNTHESIZER?** FOR UNDER $2000 ?? **THEN** WE'D BE ABLE TO DO SOME **COMMUNICATING!**

AND UNTIL THEN...?

UNTIL THEN—?

UNTIL THEN, IF YOU WANT HIGH RESOLUTION, IT PAYS TO REMEMBER THE HIGHEST-RESOLUTION COMMUNICATION TECHNIQUE OF ALL... AND IT'S AVAILABLE TODAY !!!

MEETING FACE-TO-FACE.

· EPILOGUE ·
SAY IT WITH PICTURES

TIRED OF TEXT? HERE'S
AN IMAGE GALLERY ON THE
THEME OF WORDS AND PICTURES...

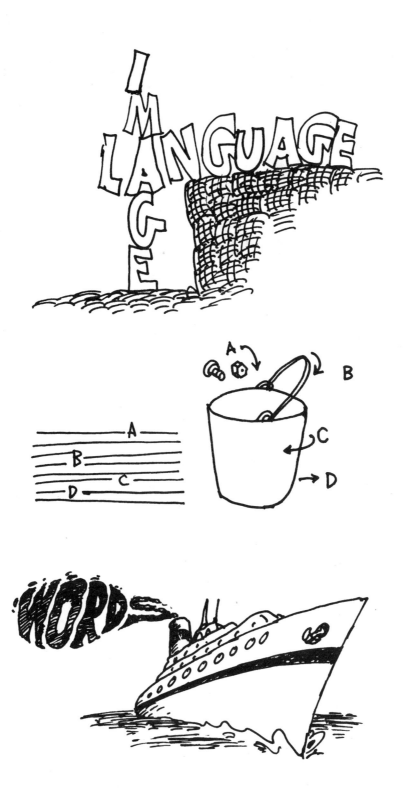

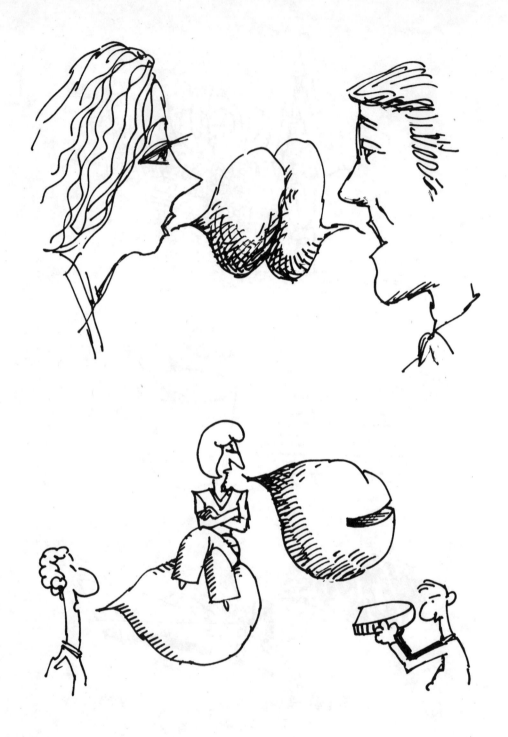

BABELIOGRAPHY

BARTHES, R., *THE SEMIOTIC CHALLENGE*, N.Y., HILL & WANG, 1988; THE HIDDEN STRUCTURE OF NARRATIVE.

BLOCK, N., ED., *IMAGERY*, CAMBRIDGE, MASS., M.I.T. PRESS, 1981; ESSAYS, PRO AND CON.

BRUNER, J., *TOWARD A THEORY OF INSTRUCTION*, CAMBRIDGE, MASS., HARVARD, 1966

BRUNER, J. + OTHERS, *STUDIES IN COGNITIVE GROWTH*, N.Y., WILEY & SONS, 1966

CHERRY, C. *ON HUMAN COMMUNICATION*, CAMBRIDGE, MASS., M.I.T., 1966; A LOOK AT INFORMATION THEORY + OTHER THINGS

CHOMSKY, N., *LANGUAGE, AND PROBLEMS OF KNOWLEDGE*, CAMBRIDGE, MASS., M.I.T., 1988; WITH EXAMPLES IN ENGLISH AND SPANISH.

ECO, U., *THE ROLE OF THE READER*, BLOOMINGTON, INDIANA, U. OF INDIANA PRESS, 1983 (?); MORE SEMIOTICS. BIFZI, BOFZI!

HAHN, M., AND SIMMEL, E., *COMMUNICATIVE BEHAVIOR AND EVOLUTION*, N.Y., ACADEMIC PRESS, 1976; PP 19-20 ARE GREAT!

HUNT, M., *THE UNIVERSE WITHIN*, N.Y., SIMON & SCHUSTER, 1982; A NICE CHAPTER ON LOGIC.

KAY., A., *COMPUTER SOFTWARE*, ARTICLE IN SCIENTIFIC AMERICAN, VOL. 251, No. 3, SEPT., 1984

McLUHAN, M., *UNDERSTANDING MEDIA*, N.Y., McGRAW-HILL, 1964; UNFASHIONABLE BUT STILL TRUE!

PAULOS, J., *I THINK, THEREFORE I LAUGH*, N.Y., COLUMBIA, 1985; EASIEST BOOK ON EPISTEMOLOGY YOU'LL EVER READ!

QUINE, W., *WORD AND OBJECT*, CAMBRIDGE, MASS., M.I.T., 1960; BRILLIANT, LAPIDARY, WITTY, UNFEELING CLASSIC

TULEJA, T., *CURIOUS CUSTOMS*, N.Y., HARMONY BOOKS, 1987; EVERYDAY RITUALS

WOLFE, J., ED., *THE MIND'S EYE*, N.Y., FREEMAN, 1986; THE ACT OF SEEING.